COLORADO SPORTS TRIVIA

Ryan O'Leary
and
J. Alexander Poulton

2011 by OverTime Books
First printed in 2011 10 9 8 7 6 5 4 3 2 1
Printed in Canada

All rights reserved. No part of this work covered by the copyrights hereon may be reproduced or used in any form or by any means—graphic, electronic or mechanical—without the prior written permission of the publisher, except for reviewers, who may quote brief passages. Any request for photocopying, recording, taping or storage on information retrieval systems of any part of this work shall be directed in writing to the publisher.

The Publisher: OverTime Books is an imprint of Éditions de la Montagne Verte

O'Leary, Ryan, 1982–
   Colorado sports trivia / Ryan O'Leary, J. Alexander Poulton.

ISBN 978-1-897277-63-8

   1. Sports—Colorado—Miscellanea. I. Poulton, J. Alexander (Jay Alexander), 1977– II. Title.

GV584.C6O54   211796.09788   C2010-907885-3

Project Director: J. Alexander Poulton
Editor: Kathy van Denderen
Cover Images: Baseball Glove © Bobbiholmes/ Dreamstime.com; Rock Climbing Gear © 2000-2009 Dreamstime/Fotofermer; Skier © iStockphoto.com/technotr; Snowboarder © Jupiterimages; Football © Toddtaulman/ Dreamstime.com; Invesco Stadium, Home of the Denver Broncos © 2000-2009 Dreamstime/Bambi L. Dingman; Coors Field, Home of the Colorado Rockies © Ffooter/Deamstime.com; Golfer © iStockphoto.com/Sergey Kashkin; Cyclist © Václav Volráb l Dreamstime.com; all other photos © Photos.com

We acknowledge the financial support of the Government of Canada through the Book Publishing Industry Development Program (BPIDP) for our publishing activities.

 Canadian Patrimoine
Heritage canadien

PC: 1

Table of Contents

Introduction **6**

Chapter 1:
    Football **9**

Chapter 2:
    Hockey **34**

Chapter 3:
    Baseball **66**

Chapter 4:
    Basketball **100**

Chapter 5:
    College Sports **111**

Chapter 6:
    Winter Sports and the Olympics **149**

Chapter 7:
    Outdoor Sports **169**

Chapter 8:
    Colorado Sports Icons **180**

Chapter 9:
    Sports Porpourri **191**

Notes on Sources **204**

Dedication

To my lovely wife, Joanna

—JAP

Acknowledgments

The road leading up to, and through a project like this is challenging, yet rewarding. Countless individuals encouraged, guided and supported my journey and will continue to do so—to them, my sincerest thanks and assurance that the love, gratitude and benevolence is fully noticed and greatly appreciated.

The biggest debt of gratitude is to my family: Mom, Dad, Andrew, Meghan, Tom and Valeria—there's no way I could have done this without you.

To my extended family, you've always been there as well, and I appreciate it. A special thanks to Uncle Bob, aka "Red," for his seemingly endless knowledge of Colorado sport and willingness to lend his expertise in crafting portions of this book.

For all of my friends, both near and far—thanks for always spurring me on.

–Ryan O'Leary

Introduction

When you come to Colorado, you arrive in a place where every sports-related musing has the potential to be fulfilled. The incomparable depth and breadth of athletic pursuit is on full display in every corner of the Centennial State—365 days a year. The extensive sport variety lends itself to the creation of indelible "trivia" moments, while fashioning some of the most intriguing sports stories and figures the world has ever known.

Colorado's most striking feature, the Rocky Mountain Range, is as grand and as magnificent as the top-level talent that emerges from it. Just ask the folks in Steamboat Springs, a tiny town nestled in the Rockies and the producer of the most Winter Olympians ever. The Rockies are also home to the world's greatest mountain bikers, cyclists, runners and endurance athletes—there's a reason Lance Armstrong races in Leadville's ultra marathon each year. For recreational athletes, the hiking trails and ski resorts are unparalleled, precisely why Lindsey Vonn makes a home in Vail. And if one mountain range

INTRODUCTION 7

isn't enough, head down to the San Juans in Colorado's southwest corner—it's where alternative sport icon Shaun White built a private, half-million-dollar snowboard halfpipe for exclusive training sessions.

For those fascinated by more traditional sport, Denver provides top-tier professional competition in all four major professional leagues. Coors Field, the site of seven National League batting titles, continually provides some of baseball's great moments, including one of the most exciting late-season World Series runs of all-time. Over at 1100 Chopper Circle, the Pepsi Center is home to the high-flying Denver Nuggets, contributors to many of the NBA's all-time high scoring records. It's also the home arena for the Colorado Avalanche, two-time Stanley Cup champions and the only team to win the Cup in its first year of existence. Across the street, the Broncos have captured the imagination of Coloradoans for more than 50 years, thanks to legendary, record-setting men like Floyd Little and John Elway.

On Colorado's college campuses, great sporting moments are the norm and not the exception. The current and historical success of Denver University's hockey and ski teams make it one of the winningest schools in Division I Athletics. Thirty miles northwest in Boulder, the Colorado Buffaloes lay claim to some of college football's greatest performances and moments, while also producing some of America's finest individual athletes. Smaller schools boast huge resumés as well—just take a look at the Colorado College Tigers' hockey team. Meanwhile, the pools at Colorado State University trained one of America's greatest Olympians, six-time gold medalist Amy Van Dyken.

Down in Colorado Springs, the United States Olympic Committee oversees amateur athletics for the entire country, continually training and sending America's elite athletes to compete against top challengers at the biggest sporting events staged worldwide. The Springs are also home to the Pikes Peak Ascent, the third oldest marathon in the country and certainly the most difficult.

The aforementioned anecdotes are just a small sampling of Colorado's many athletic offerings. The stories in this book will not only entertain you but will also leave you with several "ah-ha" moments as you discover the rich sporting history Colorado possesses.

Chapter One

Football

The First Uni's

In terms of fashion, football uniforms are hard to get wrong. The jerseys by regulation must remain simple with the player's number featured predominantly on the front and back. This leaves little room for any creative design failure. The only thing the designers must pay close attention to is color selection. Unfortunately, this is exactly where the designers for the newly formed 1960 Denver Broncos got it wrong.

To give the designers of the Broncos jersey some credit, the original choice of white, mustard yellow and brown spoke more to the landscape and history of the great state of Colorado than the bright orange and electric blue of the modern uniforms. You are more likely to see a local cowboy with brown pants and a manly yellow shirt holding a brown saddle in Colorado than someone in a bright orange and blue shirt on the street in downtown Denver. The yellow jersey and brown pants were not that bad on their own, but completing the outfit was a pair of vertical striped socks that ran to the knees and made the players' legs look like unappetizing candy stripes.

As bad as the team looked in their uniforms, they were even worse on the field. Although the Broncos won their first franchise game 13–10 over the Boston Patriots, the club won only three more games that year, finishing with a paltry 4–9–1 record. Things did not get any better the following season when the Broncos finished with a record of 3 wins and 11 losses. The Broncos needed a change to reverse their direction. They got rid of the franchise's first head coach, Frank Filchock, but something else was needed to take the team to a higher level and reconnect with fans after two abysmal years.

Management decided that the team needed a fresh look. Fans had already voiced their opinion on the uniforms by holding jersey-burning bonfires outside the stadiums. So before the start of the 1962 season, the Broncos unveiled their new orange, royal blue and white jersey accompanied by a logo that featured a bucking horse. The uniforms have changed slightly over the years, with variations in the logo, but the colors remain the same, and the people of Colorado have completely embraced the Broncos as part of their family.

Early Struggles

Originally founded as a charter member of the American Football League (AFL) in 1960, the Denver

Broncos and their faithful fans suffered through 12 years of losing football. The first decade-plus saw the Broncos post a dubious record of 53–123–6, including six double-digit loss campaigns. Mercifully in 1973, the Broncos went 7–5–2 behind veteran QB Charley Johnson—the team's first winning season after a dozen years of play. The Broncos' loss at Oakland in the season's final game cost them their first-ever visit to the playoffs, and despite posting respectable seasons thereafter, the Broncos didn't make their first playoff appearance until 1977. That year, they went all the way to the Super Bowl behind QB Craig Morton and the famed Orange Crush defense but eventually lost to the NFC Champion Dallas Cowboys 27–10 at the Superdome in New Orleans.

Rising to the Occasion

Though much of the Broncos' early existence can be aptly described as only mediocre (at least in terms of wins and losses), moments of brilliance still occurred, particularly in 1969 and 1970. One of the team's unique calling cards at that time was toppling the previous season's Super Bowl champions. Ever confident from the upset victory over the Colts in Super Bowl III, "Broadway" Joe Namath brought the New York Jets into Mile High Stadium for the second game of the 1969 season in what was expected to be a rollover victory of Denver.

With the team trailing 13–7 in the second quarter, Bronco wide receiver Mike Haffner made one of the greatest catches in team history, laying out of the back of the south end zone to corral an overthrown pass from Pete Liske with his fingertips. The highlight-reel catch amazed fans nationwide and was even featured on the *Tonight Show* with Johnny Carson. The game also featured the longest punt in AFL/NFL history as the Jets' Steve O'Neal, backed up at his own one-yard line, drove a low-trajectory howitzer over the head of the Broncos' Bill Thompson that landed at their one-yard line—a 98-yard boot that is unequalled to this day. In the end, Denver knocked off the previous year's champs 21–19.

The following season, Denver repeated their Goliath-slaying ways against rival Kansas City at Mile High Stadium in early October 1970. That day, the Broncos handled their AFC foes by a score of 26–13, propelling the team to a surprising 3–0 for the first time in franchise history. Alas, the Broncos only mustered two more victories throughout the remainder of the 1970 campaign, finishing 5–8–1.

When the AFL and NFL merged in 1970, Cleveland Browns owner Art Modell vehemently opposed the move, exclaiming, "The Denver Broncos will never play in my stadium." A year later, Denver marched into Cleveland Stadium and handed the Browns a 27–0 loss in front of Modell and 75,000 dismayed supporters. The Bronco win was bolstered by a touchdown from former Colorado Buffalo star Bobby Anderson and 113 rushing yards by Floyd

Little. Although the win wasn't against a former Super Bowl victor, it was a point of pride for a Bronco fan base grasping for positive moments throughout the team's tumultuous run from 1960 to 1972.

Little Big Man

Also lost in the shuffle of 12-straight losing seasons was running back Floyd Little, arguably the greatest at his position during his era and the franchise's best until Terrell Davis emerged 20 years later. Floyd came to the Broncos via a first-round draft pick in 1967 from a Syracuse pedigree that boasted the likes of Jim Brown and Ernie "The Elmira Express" Davis.

From 1968 to 1973, Little led the league in rushing in only one season (1133 yards in 1971), however, his accumulated rushing total (5566 yards) over those six years was the best in football. In fact, during his nine-year career, all with Denver, Little amassed the most all-purpose yards in professional football and finished behind only O.J. Simpson in rushing over that span. The New Haven, Connecticut, native is also one of three players in NFL history to combine 6000 career-rushing yards with 3000 career special-teams yards. At the time he retired in 1975, Little was the seventh leading rusher in professional football history. Little's career statistics are as follows:

- 117 career games
- 1643 rushes for 6323 yards with 43 touchdowns

- 215 receptions for 2418 yards with nine touchdowns
- 104 kickoff returns for 2523 yards
- 81 punt returns for 893 yards with two touchdowns

The most striking notion that emerges when considering Little's accomplishments is that he was the only offensive weapon for the Broncos during the era. Opposing defenses, and everyone else in the stadium for that matter, knew that the ball would be handed to Little, and the Broncos' leading man was singled out in every contest. Little overcame this disadvantage to generate 61 career games with at least 100 combined yards—the most in pro football during his career and in Broncos' history.

For his accomplishments, Broncos' fans dubbed Little "The Franchise" because he single-handedly kept the Broncos in Denver when the team's less-than-stellar on-field performance threatened to have them moved elsewhere.

Obviously, Little was respected in Denver and by Bronco fans everywhere, but throughout his career and the years following his retirement, his talents were largely overlooked. For 30 years NFL Hall of Fame voters disregarded Little's career, which left him wondering if the day would ever come when he would enter football's most exclusive fraternity. Finally, in 2010, after years of torment and dejection, Little was elected into the Hall of Fame alongside fellow inductees Russ Grimm, Rickey Jackson, Emmitt

Smith, Dick LeBeau, John Randle and Jerry Rice. The NFL's Gil Brandt wrote of Little's induction, "He was a truly great ball carrier in his prime; had he played for a contender, he might have been one of the most exciting players in history. While that's speculation and can be argued either way, his induction into the Hall of Fame solidifies a legacy of greatness that can never be taken away."

Orange Crush

This is not just a refreshing drink. In the 1970s, the Denver Broncos had one of the league's most devastating defensive lines that featured such notables as linebackers Randy Gradishar and Tom Jackson, linemen Barney Chavous, Lyle Alzado and Rubin Carter, among others. Through much of the mid-to-late 1970s, the Broncos defensive line had been the terror of the league, crushing quarterbacks and running backs who dared venture across their lines. It was largely because of the "Orange Crush" that the Broncos made it into the 1977 Super Bowl, unfortunately only to lose to the Dallas Cowboys. The name came from the orange uniforms and the unique crushing the line inflicted on opponents.

The Halo Spinner

The Orange Crush as a unit garnered much fanfare for their intimidating ways, but nobody on the front line was more menacing or punitive than Rich "Tombstone" Jackson. Considered the greatest defensive lineman "most NFL fans may never have heard about," Jackson gashed and bashed opposing offensive lines for the Denver Broncos from 1967 to 1971. With little other on-field entertainment coming from the Broncos, fans paid particular attention to the number of offensive linemen "Tombstone" sent to the sidelines after falling victim to his punishing "head slap," or as some called it, "halo spinner." One head slap that was particularly famous among Bronco fans was when Jackson's hand literally broke Bill Hayhoe's helmet during a game against the Green Bay Packers.

Jackson's talents extended beyond his patented move, as he accumulated 43 career sacks, enjoying 10 in both 1968 and 1970, and a career high 11 in 1969. Each of those three campaigns earned him a Pro Bowl appearance and First Team All-Pro honors. Unfortunately for Jackson and the Bronco franchise, a severe knee injury forced the All-Pro to end his career abruptly after the 1972 season. As a fitting homage to Jackson, *Sports Illustrated*'s football expert, "Dr. Z," Paul Zimmerman, described him as the "finest overall defensive end and pass rusher" he ever saw and "a surefire hall of famer" had Jackson's career lasted longer.

Taking the Long Route

The Denver Bronco name is synonymous with that of John Elway—the greatest and most recognizable figure the organization has ever known.

FOOTBALL 17

The Bronco faithful can readily recount Elway's "Mile High Magic" moments hearkening back to the successful days of yesteryear, but few can recite the details of the unorthodox manner in which the Broncos acquired their future star.

A two-sport star in high school, Elway was included in *Parade Magazine*'s All-American High School Team and was also recognized for his baseball talent, being drafted by the Kansas City Royals in 1979. Despite offers from the major leagues and 60 other schools, the highly sought-after Elway elected to enroll at Stanford University in California's Bay Area, where he starred on both the football and baseball fields. Elway was by far the best player on those Stanford Cardinal teams from 1979 to 1982, and although the team struggled on the field with a mediocre 20–23 record and zero bowl appearances, the results could have been much worse. When he graduated, Elway's name was littered throughout the Stanford and Pac-10 record books, holding nearly every passing and total-offense mark.

Furthermore, Elway's college days also featured an appearance in one of college football's most memorable games. During the 1982 edition of "The Game" against the rival California Bears, Elway completed a 29-yard pass on fourth-and-17 late in the fourth quarter, trailing 19–17. The amazing play set up what seemed to be a 52-yard game-winning field goal by Mark Harmon, with four seconds remaining in the contest. What happened on the ensuing kickoff is quite familiar to sports fans—the numerous laterals, missed tackles, "the band is on the field" and a shocking 25–20 Cal win. Although "The Play" is usually associated with the man who scored the touchdown (Kevin Moen) and the trombone player who was pasted (Gary Tyrrell), it was Elway's effort that made the play possible. For Elway, however, the play was memorable for a different reason—it cost him the Heisman Trophy and a trip to a bowl game. Elway contended that "...the referees ruined [his] final college football game" after they allowed the touchdown to stand despite controversy over the laterals and the Stanford Band interfering with the play.

On the heels of the bitter defeat experienced during his final college football game, Elway made himself eligible for the 1983 NFL draft, but it came with stipulations. Everyone involved with the draft knew the Baltimore Colts would take Elway with the first overall pick, much to the distaste of the quarterback who believed the team could not provide him a real chance at success. Elway protested, threatening to play professional baseball instead of ever taking a snap in Baltimore.

In fact, Elway was redrafted into Major League Baseball in 1981 and played the following two summers in the Yankees' farm system. Out of fear that his team's first-pick opportunity would prove fruitless, Colts' owner Robert Irsay obliged Elway and traded him to the Denver Broncos on May 2, 1983, for quarterback Mark Herrmann, rights to offensive lineman Chris Hinton and a first-round pick, offensive guard Ron Solt in the 1984 NFL draft. It was a small price to pay for a two-time Super Bowl Champion and future NFL Hall of Famer.

The Drive

Any football fan old enough will remember that fateful night on January 11, 1987, when the Denver Broncos went on a 98-yard end-to-end rush in the AFC Championship game against the Cleveland Browns with minutes left on the clock. And for those of you who might be too young to remember or perhaps were not even around for the momentous event, it's an honor to relay one of the most exciting moments in Colorado pro football history.

The Denver Broncos had been to the Super Bowl just once in their history prior to the 1986 season playoffs, ultimately losing out to the Dallas Cowboys. Since 1960, Broncos fans had been patiently waiting for their team to reach a level of skill where they could compete season to season. By 1986, all those pieces seemed to come together, led by the golden arm of Broncos quarterback John Elway. Going into the 1986 season playoffs, the Broncos were not the favorites to win the championship, but with a little luck and grit, they could surprise.

Their first challenge came from the New England Patriots in the AFC Divisional playoffs. The game was tight, but Elway managed to run in a touchdown of his own in the later stages of the game, and defensive lineman Rulon Jones then sacked New England quarterback Tony Eason in his own end zone for the two-point safety just as the Patriots were trying to start a drive of their own. The game ended by a score of 22–17, and the Broncos moved into the AFC Championship against the Cleveland Browns.

John Elway, Renaissance Man

Not only can John Elway win Super Bowls, act in popular television shows, help out his community and be a well-rounded father, but he also can kick butt in a stock car going over 150 miles per hour.

We all know about the John Elway who executed "The Drive" and brought the Super Bowl to Denver, but few know anything else about the man. Before he began his professional football career, he almost made a career out of baseball playing on the Stanford University team. But to peg this athlete as a one-dimensional jock would be presumptuous. Although he did devote a major amount of his time to becoming the greatest quarterback in Colorado sports history, and arguably the greatest in the NFL, Elway is a man of varied tastes and interests. Once he had achieved his goal of making it into the world of professional football, he always found time to give back to his fans and to those in need within his community.

Elway has given his time and money to many local charities and is an active supporter of the Make-a-Wish Foundation and the Muhammad Ali Parkinson Center. He also has his own personal charity, the John Elway Heroes Foundation, which was formed to provide support and funding for exemplary Americans and members of the military who have given back to their fellow man and defended the country's freedom. When he first started the foundation in 1987, Elway wanted to focus on the community that had shown him so much support, especially the kids who looked up to him. Although his exploits could fill an entire book, the man John Elway does not stop there.

John Elway, Business Man

Since leaving behind his professional football career, Elway has branched out into the world of business with several ventures, most notably as a co-owner of the Colorado Crush of the Arena Football League. Jumping on board in 2002, Elway's fame helped to bring a new level of attention to the fledgling league, and in 2007 he was named to the league's executive committee. Although the Broncos have not won a Super Bowl since Elway retired, he helped to bring the Arena League title to Denver in 2005 when his Colorado Crush defeated the Georgia Force by a score of 51–48. However, because of financial issues and lack of agreement within the AFL ownership group, the league was suspended in 2009 and the Colorado Crush were folded. Since then, the AFL has returned to operations, but Elway and the Crush have been left in the dustbin of sports history. However, hold off on the tears for Elway's failed business venture, because the former football player has thrown his hat into a variety of arenas.

In 1997, Elway sold five of his eight auto dealerships for an estimated $82 million. If that isn't enough, he ventured into the culinary arts world when he opened a steakhouse named Elway's, one in the upscale Cherry Creek shopping district and another in the Ritz-Carleton Hotel in downtown Denver. When he finds the time, he writes a blog on NFL.com and often does commentary on Broncos games for television and radio.

Elway also dabbled in the thespian arts, appearing in several commercials and television shows; he even had his own video game, "John Elway's Quarterback," for the Nintendo Entertainment System.

We can certainly expect to see more of John Elway, who has just reached his 50s, even though it was 1998 that he last suited up for the Denver Broncos.

Elway Helps Out

Joshua Vannoy was a die-hard Denver Broncos fan and was not one bit ashamed to flaunt his support for his favorite team. But that enthusiasm for the Broncos got the Pennsylvania high school student into hot water two days before the 2006 AFC Championship game pitting the Broncos up against the hometown favorite Pittsburgh Steelers.

Vannoy knew that by wearing his Denver Broncos Elway jersey to school that day he would receive some unwanted attention from fellow classmates and that it would be all in good fun, but then he walked into his ethnic relations class. His teacher John Kelly, himself a rabid Steelers fan, decided to have a little fun with Vannoy and forced him to sit on the floor for the duration of a mid-term exam while his classmates laughed at him. Normally a straight "A" student, Vannoy could not concentrate on the exam under the stressful circumstances and ended up failing. But the mocking did not end there.

Word of Vannoy's support for the Broncos spread throughout the school, and as a result, he became the target of jokes and insults that progressively escalated to the point where Vannoy stopped attending school and eventually transferred to another school. The teacher claimed that it was a lesson on ethnic discrimination for Vannoy and the class that unfortunately got out of hand. When Elway got wind of the incident, he had a custom-designed recliner with heat and massage sent to the Vannoy household so that Joshua could sit in comfort and watch the Broncos game on TV. Unfortunately, the Steelers won the game 34–17.

Elway Gets Hosed

No one is perfect. Not even John Elway. For years it seemed as if the poster boy of Broncos history could do no wrong in his business dealings. He had made millions from his car dealerships and from lending his name to various companies as a promotional tool and had also led a successful charity. But in 2010, Elway—the man with the golden business touch—was taught a nasty lesson when he lost a reported $15 million in an investment scheme.

Elway and a business partner had placed $15 million of their hard-earned money into a hedge fund where their investor, a man named Sean Mueller, allegedly used the funds for his own personal dealings. In October 2010, Mueller was arrested on charges of racketeering, securities fraud and theft.

The Barrel Man

Former United Airlines mechanic Tim McKernan was just an average guy who loved football and was passionate about the Denver Broncos. He had gone to every home game since 1967. But simply attending the games wasn't enough for McKernan, and in 1977 he bet his brother $10 that he could get on television by wearing a barrel. After painting a barrel the color of an Orange Crush soda can, he attached a pair of leather straps to act as suspenders, slid into the barrel without a shirt, put on an orange cowboy hat and went to watch the Broncos game. He won the bet and decided to wear the barrel to every game thereafter. He soon became the most recognized fan in the NFL and the Broncos' most popular mascot.

"He liked the attention, he loved inspiring the fans and had a take-charge attitude," said Tim's son, Todd McKernan, who said he was 17 when his dad first donned the costume.

In 2003, Tim suffered an aneurysm and was confined to a wheelchair and placed on oxygen. But the tough Bronco fan recovered and returned to his spot in the stands. His health issues again caught up with him, and in 2007, the Broncos retired his barrel and Tim received a special thank you from the organization during a halftime ceremony where he was presented with a team football and received an ovation from the crowd that left him in tears. Tim McKernan died in December 2009 at the age of 69.

Mile High Salute

The elation accompanied by a Broncos touchdown is usually followed by another indelible moment for fans, namely the "Mile High Salute." The move was started by the Broncos' former star running back, Terrell Davis; when Bronco players reach the end zone, they immediately turn and face the crowd and honor them with a military-style salute. During Davis' seven years with the Broncos, the salute was seen quite frequently as he tallied 67 total touchdowns and won two Super Bowls with Denver. In fact, Davis was given the nickname "T.D." because of his initials and in reference to his prolific touchdown haul. At the time of his retirement in 2002, Davis stood first in Bronco history in rushing yards (7607) and second in touchdowns (65)—records that still stand to this day. Davis had a three-year stretch from 1996 to 1998 when he scored 53 touchdowns and rushed for a dumbfounding 5298 yards—including

23 touchdowns and 2008 yards in 1998, finishing atop the NFL in both categories. Though Davis hasn't saluted a Bronco crowd since he last scored a touchdown in 2000, Bronco players continue to perpetuate a great Bronco tradition.

Unlikely Tandem

Accolades are often reserved for John Elway and Terrell Davis when describing Denver's impressive stretch (39–9) and back-to-back Super Bowls from 1996 to 1998, but two of the Broncos' greatest offensive talents in franchise history are sometimes overlooked. As a tight end, Shannon Sharpe embodied a pure offensive weapon not typically seen at the position until his arrival. The man whose tongue was equally as sharp as his route-running transformed the tight-end position during his 14 years in a Denver Bronco and Baltimore Raven uniform. By the time all was said and done (and a lot was said on his part), Sharpe had obliterated all previously held records at the position, thus creating a new standard for the next generation of NFL tight ends. Sharpe was the first tight end to reach 10,000 yards receiving (10,060), finishing more than 2000 receiving yards ahead of the previous record holder (Ozzie Newsome at 7980). Sharpe's career marks of 815 receptions and 62 touchdowns positioned him first among tight ends when he retired. Currently, Sharpe stands second in all three categories as he has since been usurped by Tony Gonzalez.

A deeper look into Sharpe's career reveals even more about one of the NFL's truly great players. While with the Broncos, Sharpe blocked for six separate 1000-yard rushers culminating in nine 1000-yard seasons (Bobby Humphrey, Gaston Green, Terrell Davis, Olandis Gary, Clinton Portis, Jamal Lewis). Other accomplishments of note include 60 or more catches in 10 of his last 11 seasons, three 1000-yard receiving seasons and the record for most receiving yards (214) by a tight end in a single game (against Kansas City on October 20, 2002). Most importantly, Sharpe's three Super Bowl rings, coupled with a 13–5 playoff record, solidify his status as a bona fide winner at the NFL level. Leave it to the loquacious and self-aggrandizing Sharpe to put his achievements in perspective: "Ditka and Chester and Ozzie, they got the opportunity to beat up on linebackers and safeties. They covered me with their No. 1 cornerback. That's the kind of respect they pay Tony Gonzalez. That's the ultimate respect."

Iron Rod

Flanking Shannon Sharpe for all those years was Rod Smith, who can only be characterized as the opposite of Sharpe in terms of personality; he presents a quieter but equally successful approach to the game. Smith's entrance into the NFL as an undrafted free agent served as an omen for his future as an unheralded, off-the-radar-screen star wide receiver. The consummate team player, Smith is the all-time receiving leader in Broncos history with 11,389 yards, and for his efforts was named to the Pro Bowl three times during his 14-year career. When asked about his franchise receiving record, Smith remained true to his humble nature: "I really don't want to talk about me. I didn't want to talk about me last week, and I don't this week. I want to talk about our team."

The Broncos' success in the mid to late 1990s would have been impossible without Smith, but he was always quick to deflect attention away from himself. The media treated him as such and that's why many aren't familiar with his numerous achievements. For example, Smith is Denver's all-time leader in yards from scrimmage, receptions, receiving yards and receiving touchdowns. And of all the undrafted players in history, he is the only one to accumulate 10,000 receiving yards. He leads all undrafted wide receivers in history in catches (849), receiving yards (11,389) and touchdown receptions (68). Smith's numbers are emphatic evidence that he let his play do all the talking.

All You Can Handle

Brandon Marshall's four years with the Denver Broncos were tenuous to say the least—full of ups and downs—but his on-field talent was unquestioned. Just one year after being drafted out of Central Florida in 2006, Marshall became one of the league's elite receivers and the main target of both his quarterbacks and opposing secondaries alike. Marshall's

6-foot-4-inch, 240-pound frame, combined with elite-level speed and magnetic hands, currently make him one of the NFL's best pass catchers—talent that was on full display on December 13, 2009, on the road against the Indianapolis Colts.

In a 28–16 loss, Marshall set the NFL's all-time record for most receptions in a game when he caught 21 Kyle Orton passes. The 21 receptions went along with 200 receiving yards, a career-high, and two touchdowns. Marshall broke Terrell Owens' NFL single-game record of 20 grabs—set in 2000 when he was a member of the San Francisco 49ers in a December game against the Chicago Bears. In terms of the Broncos franchise, Marshall broke his own record of 18 receptions, which he accomplished on September 14, 2008, against the San Diego Chargers. That performance came in Marshall's first game back from a three-game suspension handed down by the NFL stemming from "off-the-field issues." Marshall's imprint on the record book isn't just limited to a single night in Indianapolis. He also posted three-straight 100-reception seasons from 2007 to 2009, making him one of five players in NFL history to accomplish the feat.

Denver Broncos Facts

- Former Broncos kicker Jason Elam is tied for the longest field goal (63 yards) in NFL history. He also holds the record for most seasons (16) with 100 or more points.

- John Elway holds the NFL record for most times sacked in a career (516). He is also ranked third all-time in passes attempted (7250), yards gained (51,475) and seasons with 3000 or more yards thrown (12).

- The franchise holds the record for most points overcome (31) to tie a ball game. The team trailed Buffalo 38–7 on November 27, 1960, and the game finished with the teams deadlocked at 38 apiece.

- Of the eight original founding American Football League teams, only the Denver Broncos and Buffalo Bills have never moved from their original city.

- Former Dallas Cowboys star running back Tony Dorsett finished his Hall of Fame career with the Broncos.

- From 1998 to 2006, the Broncos had eight seasons with a running back rushing for over 1000 yards. Those eight 1000-yard seasons were accomplished by six different running backs: Terrell Davis, Olandis Gary, Mike Anderson, Clinton Portis, Reuben Droughns and Tatum Bell.

FOOTBALL

- The Broncos were the first American pro football club to employ an African American place kicker, Gene Mingo.

- Former Broncos head coach Mike Shanahan was a promising football star in high school and college, but during a practice he was hit hard and ruptured his kidneys, causing his heart to stop for 30 seconds, nearly killing him.

- In the years 1960 through 1980, the Broncos had eight different head coaches. Since 1981 (through 2008), the team had only three different head coaches.

- In a Thanksgiving game against the New York Giants on November 26, 2009, Broncos head coach Josh McDaniels was caught on national television screaming at his offensive line during a break after they had committed three false starts. He screamed, "All we're trying to do is win a F#$@$@ game!" The profane words were broadcast on the NFL Network. The words did have some effect on the Broncos as they ended up winning the game 26–6.

- The first former Broncos player elected to the Hall of Fame was cornerback Willie Brown who played with the team from 1963 to 1966.

- Pittsburgh Steeler Ben Roethlisberger wears the number 7 in honor of his hero John Elway.

- In a 1994 episode of the television sitcom Home Improvement, John Elway guest starred as himself, helping the show's star character, Tim

"The Toolman" Taylor, build a house for Habitat for Humanity. Also helping out were former Detroit Lions quarterback Eric Hipple, Green Bay Packers defensive end Sean Jones, former New York Jets quarterback Ken O'Brien, and boxer Evander Holyfield.

- Although John Elway was the picture of professionalism on and off the field, his personal life has taken a hit since his retirement. He lost his father to a heart attack in 2001 and his twin sister to cancer in 2002. To make matters worse, just one year later he divorced his wife Janet Buchan. Elway's personal life has been looking a little brighter since that string of bad years, and he married former Oakland Raiders cheerleader Paige Green in August 2009.

- The Broncos have retired three numbers: John Elway (7), Frank Tripucka (18) and Floyd Little (44).

Denver Football Quotations

"How ironic, to be my last game that I ever played would be against Dan [Reeves] in a Super Bowl. The thing I always was afraid of was playing in a Super Bowl when it was raining. I can't throw a wet ball."

"I've always joked about Joe Montana not appreciating his Super Bowls nearly as much as I do because he never lost one. We lost three before we got one."

"I've experienced the highest of highs and lowest of lows. I think to really appreciate anything you have to be at both ends of the spectrum."

–John Elway

"The one thing that scares me the most is failing. It scares me that one day I won't be at this level. But while I'm here and while I'm having success early, I'm trying to do everything to stay on this level."

"You can be the best person in the league but if you don't win championships, something's missing."

–Terrell Davis

"If you're not improving…chances are you're not going to win."

–Former Denver Broncos coach Mike Shanahan

Chapter Two

Hockey

The Early Teams

Anecdotal evidence suggests hockey was played in Leadville, Colorado, in 1901 between the Whites and the Maroons. The *Denver Times* reported that 27 individuals constituted the Leadville Hockey Club, which divided itself into separate sides (White and Maroon) and played matches on a frequent basis. A typical season between the two lasted until April, when the team with the most wins throughout the season was awarded the Silver and Gold Cup. No further details are known, but the report from the *Denver Times* (published December 24, 1901) gives a clear indication of hockey taking a footing in Colorado.

Professional hockey in Colorado began in 1950 when the Denver Falcons of the United States Hockey League (USHL) came to town. In later years, unsuccessful professional hockey franchises such as the Denver Mavericks and Invaders called Colorado's capital home, but only for a short time. Not until

1968 did a lasting tradition of high-level hockey come to Colorado.

The Denver Spurs

Denver's first true taste of professional hockey came with the arrival of the Denver Spurs in 1968. The team played its home games at the Denver Coliseum (still standing today) and competed in the Western Hockey League (WHL). The first season was an inauspicious start for the Spurs, who churned out a record of just 23–44–7, finishing dead last in the WHL. In fact, the Spurs started the season 0–9 and didn't earn the franchise's first victory until November 2, 1968, against the Vancouver Canucks. Spurs head coach Rudy Pilous changed netminders for the game and started 21-year-old Rocky Farr instead of veteran Jacques Caron—a decision that proved fruitful for Pilous and the Spurs.

Farr surrendered a goal on the first shot he faced just one minute into the tilt, but that was all the scoring the Canucks would muster. Gordon Vejprava and John Rodgers each scored a goal in the second period, and with time waning in the third period, the Spurs' faithful, numbering 3000, went into a frenzy celebrating the team's first victory, a 2–1 final. It was Farr who time and time again stood on his head and single-handedly won games that first season. At the end of the year, fans voted Farr the "Most Popular Spurs' Player."

In subsequent seasons, gains in the standings were hard to come by, but those years served as building blocks for future success, finally realized during the 1971–72 WHL campaign. The Spurs found victory through the likes of forwards Fran Huck, Gary Veneruzzo and Ron Buchanan—accounting for one-third of the team's points that season. Bob Johnson backstopped the Spurs and was a perfect compliment to a team that had suddenly become an offensive force. Denver finished first in the WHL after the regular season, a full 11 points clear of second place Phoenix. Although the Spurs earned home-ice advantage in the first round of the playoffs, they had to travel to San Diego because the Ice Capades had claimed rights to the Coliseum.

Nonetheless, Denver quickly disposed of the Gulls in a sweep, setting up the Lester Patrick Cup final against Portland. The series with the Buckaroos lasted just five games, and Denver emerged the victor behind the fortified wall known as Bob Johnson. The Spurs' goaltender went a robust 4–1 with a 1.00 goals-against average and two shutouts in the postseason (this same Bob Johnson is the father of current NHL goaltender, Brent Johnson, of the Pittsburgh Penguins). As a result of winning the WHL title, the Denver Spurs handed the state of Colorado its first professional championship of any kind.

Two seasons later in 1974, the WHL closed its doors because of the burgeoning World Hockey Association (WHA) and the long-standing National

Hockey League (NHL) digging their heels into traditional markets and snatching top talent away from lesser leagues. Additionally, the NHL granted Denver and Seattle "conditional" charters as NHL clubs (although they never joined), which applied even more pressure on the WHL. Subsequently, Denver played one year in the Central Hockey League (CHL) before joining the WHA in 1975.

The 1975–76 Denver Spurs of the WHA failed to imprint themselves into the consciousness of the city's populace—just 5000 fans saw the team's opening game against the Houston Aeros (featuring Gordie Howe in his 29th professional season). Despite this failure to draw spectators, it showed that the club was ready for professional hockey, but only if it was of the right brand. Prior to the arrival of the Spurs, there had been vocal support for bringing an NHL franchise to the city, and with each passing year, those voices had reached the right ears to the point where it wasn't a matter of whether Denver would get a team but when.

On average, only 3000 fans came to support the Spurs at the newly built McNichols Sports Arena, which had a capacity of 16,800. The Spurs had no hope for survival because the WHA had been branded as the lesser league when compared with the pedigree of the NHL. As a result, few fans showed up to the Spurs games and the team folded at the end of their inaugural season.

The Most Telling of Anthems

The sale of the Spurs will live in lore for years to come because of the comical way in which the players learned of the franchise's departure from Denver. Spurs' owner Ivan Mullenix secretively brokered a deal to move the Spurs to Ottawa, where they would be branded as the "Civics," on January 2, 1976. Mullenix never told his players about the deal, and the league never made a formal announcement until 15 days later, on January 17. Spurs players received wind of the impending move during the pre-game ceremonies of their next road game. While standing proud in their Denver uniforms, the players heard the melody of "O Canada" reverberating throughout the arena—and only then did the Spurs realize their days in Denver had come to a bitter conclusion.

The Colorado Rockies

Although it was a short-lived affair, Denver's first taste of the NHL brand of hockey began nearly two decades prior to the current franchise with the arrival of the Colorado Rockies.

Born out of the demise of the Kansas City Scouts, the Colorado Rockies were the second attempt at bringing professional hockey to the Mile High City. By bringing in an NHL franchise, the ownership group hoped the new Colorado Rockies would bring in the fans and the money. All that was needed was a winning team to ease its way into the hearts, minds and wallets of the fans.

The hopes for the team's success on the ice were tempered yet positive that in a few short years the club would be capable of challenging in the playoffs, but from the outset, prospects did not look good.

In their six seasons in the league, the Rockies boasted a wealth of talent that included such NHL alumni as Lanny McDonald, Wilf Paiement, René Robert, Rob Ramage and Steve Tambellini but the team never managed to find the right balance of chemistry and depth to take the franchise very far. The first season was a disaster on the ice and in the stands. The Rockies only managed to win 20 games, and fewer fans ventured out to see the team with each passing game. Despite posting their worst record during the 1977–1978 season, the Rockies limped into the playoffs because all other teams in their division performed so poorly.

The Rockies squandered the gift in the first round of the playoffs, taken out in consecutive games with barely a whimper. The team's management tried to bring some semblance of a fighting spirit by hiring the infamous and flamboyant head coach Don Cherry. Before the start of the season, Cherry made waves with a few comments that riled up the Denver hockey faithful. In a local commercial aired by Rockies' management, Cherry said, "I'll tell you one thing, we're going to be tough." This led to the Rockies' 1979–80 motto of, "Come to the fights and see a Rockies Game break out!" It was a message that was seen on billboards throughout the Denver metro area. Cherry also publicly promised to throw the Rockies a party after their 16th victory, one more than the team had managed the season earlier. Even with the promise and hype created by Don Cherry's arrival, the Rockies' 16th win did not come until their 59th game, on February 22, 1980.

In his first season as head coach, Cherry knew he had a decent team upfront but that they struggled in goal with their netminders. True to form, Cherry went so far as to call his own European goaltender, Hardy Astrom, the "Swedish Sieve." After Astrom's particularly poor performance in goal, Cherry reportedly told him, "If I had a gun, I'd shoot you." Cherry had asked management to find him a new goaltender, but general manager Ray Miron would not make a trade. By the end of the 1979–80 season, it was pretty clear that Cherry was not going to be with the team any longer, and in his final game, he was part of one of the most memorable job exits in history.

The Rockies' final game that season would serve as a resounding sendoff for their head coach. Denver was caught in a blizzard, but 12,000 fans (many more than average) came out to see the final act of the year. Cherry showed up for his final game in Denver wearing a cowboy hat and boots, and after the final horn sounded the end of the game, his players formed two lines on the ice, raised their sticks above their heads forming an arch and Cherry paraded through waving and blowing kisses to the

HOCKEY   41

cheering crowd. Cherry said goodbye to the Rockies and a few years later so would the people of Denver.

Rockies' management did not formally release Cherry until six weeks after the conclusion of the 1979–80 season, but being fired turned out to be a blessing for Cherry. During the NHL playoffs that season, *Hockey Night in Canada* hired Cherry to provide color for broadcasts. To this day, 30 years on, Cherry is a fixture on the show, providing commentary each week in a segment called "The Coach's Corner," and he is viewed as one of the most recognizable hockey analysts in the world. Cherry's celebrity status is best explained by Joel Darling, executive director of *Hockey Night in Canada,* "It's a real hard thing to describe. He's the most recognized face in Canada. It's like traveling with a rock star, the Rolling Stones, except he's bigger than them in this country." Ironically, none of Cherry's current success would have been possible without his dismal coaching performance and release from the Rockies.

Hockey fans in the city craved a competitive team, and they kept showing up for games, but more often than not they left the arena disappointed. The Rockies' faithful knew that NHL hockey in Denver could only last so long because the team was constantly changing ownership. Finally, in 1982, New Jersey shipping millionaire John McMullen bought out the struggling franchise and moved them to the Meadowlands Arena where they were rechristened the

New Jersey Devils for the start of the 1982–83 season. The team received its name after more than 10,000 fans voted for the name of "Devils," a reference to a threatening mythological creature known as the "Jersey Devil," which supposedly roamed the Pine Barrens of southern New Jersey.

A Brief History of the Quebec Nordiques

To understand the origins of the Colorado Avalanche, we first must look back in time to their ancestral franchise that entered the NHL in 1979 after a failed stint in the defunct World Hockey Association (along with the Edmonton Oilers, the Hartford Whalers and the Winnipeg Jets).

The Nordiques were one of the better teams from the WHA, previously winning the WHA Avco Cup championship in 1977. When the decision was made to switch the franchise over to the NHL, the Nordiques players were well acquainted with each other and played a solid style of hockey, but in joining the NHL, the players were forced into a dispersal draft, and the team had to rebuild from the bottom up. The Nordiques languished at the bottom of the league for several years as a result and struggled to find their place in the new NHL.

The 1980s was a decade with many milestones for the franchise as they altered their lineup of players, coaches and general managers, all looking for that magic that can bring success on the ice and in the playoffs. Through it all, the Nordiques battled their provincial rival Montreal Canadiens, and by the time 1990 arrived, the club had firmly established an identity of its own, but the Stanley Cup still remained out of reach. Even with legendary players like Michel Goulet and brothers Peter and Anton Stastny, the Nordiques could not make it far into the playoffs. The Nordiques' base of star players had aged, and management sought a new direction and a player with which to build on for the future. The player who took over the lead of the team from Goulet and the Stastny brothers was none other than a young Joe Sakic.

Since joining the Nordiques for his first season in 1988–89, the rookie had established himself as the potential leader of the club with 62 points in his first year followed by a sophomore season of 102 points. But the Nordiques continued to struggle early on in the 1990s and needed an influx of new blood to turn the franchise's fortunes around. Sakic was indeed the core of the new team, and the management looked to add talent around him. After finishing at the bottom of the standings in 1991, the Nordiques used their first overall pick to select Eric Lindros as part of their future plans. However, this would not be the case as Lindros refused to play for the Nordiques, forcing management to trade him before he even played a single game in the league.

At first, the fans were devastated at losing the scoring potential of such a talented young rookie, but when the Nordiques sent Lindros to the Philadelphia

Flyers in exchange for Peter Forsberg, Mike Ricci, Ron Hextall, Steve Duchesne and Kerry Huffman, they were establishing the base of the team that would eventually go on to win the Stanley Cup.

By the 1992–1993 season, the fortunes of the team on the ice began to change. The club added talented forwards Mats Sundin and Adam Deadmarsh, taking the team from the second-worst record in the league to the fourth best at the end of 1993. But while the team progressed on the ice, the economic realities of small-market Canadian teams began to weigh on the owners, and despite the team's popularity with its fan base, the franchise was losing money.

The league's Canadian teams had been struggling to keep pace with their American counterparts in the age of rising player salaries, the weakening Canadian dollar, and the NHL head office push for teams to build new arenas. The new era of the NHL could no longer support the Nordiques in Quebec, and in 1995, after the team was eliminated from the playoffs, the franchise packed up and started the 1995–96 season as the Colorado Avalanche.

The Birth of the Avalanche

Having twice failed to establish professional hockey in a few decades (The Denver Spurs of the WHA in 1976 and the Colorado Rockies from 1976 to 1982), the NHL was wary of returning their brand of hockey to the Mile High City. But Denver had a loyal, knowledgeable fan base among a growing population, so reservations were put aside and, in 1995, the COMSAT Entertainment Group announced on July 1, 1995, that they had purchased the Quebec Nordiques and were moving the club to Denver to play as the Colorado Avalanche.

A logo composed of a burgundy-colored letter "A" with an avalanche of snow wrapped around it in the shape of the letter "C" was chosen to represent the team. An alternate logo of a Sasquatch footprint can be seen on the shoulders of the team's home and away jerseys. The Sasquatch logo was chosen because the mythical creature is purportedly often sighted in Colorado's vast forests and mountains, according to many witnesses over the years.

The First Year

The good news for the newly branded Colorado Avalanche was that their ancestral franchise was stocked with a lineup of high-quality players. By the time the Nordiques became the Avalanche, they had built up a roster of current and future stars that included Joe Sakic, Peter Forsberg, Scott Young, Owen Nolan and rookie goaltender Jocelyn Thibault, all of whom were competitive enough to avoid the dreaded expansion team curse that many new franchises go through for years. Although expansion teams like the Ottawa Senators and the Tampa Bay Lightning went through several years of building through the draft and smart trades, the Avalanche hit the ice at the start of the 1995–96 season with a fully rounded team that had excellent chemistry.

The season began with promise, and the people of Denver generously embraced their new team, selling out the first handful of games at home. The Avalanche were a good team, but they were still far from competing with the more elite teams of the league such as the New Jersey Devils and the Detroit Red Wings. The Avalanche had a solid team upfront with plenty of scoring power, but their goaltending remained the weak link. Young goaltender Thibault had shown flashes of brilliance, and Stéphane Fiset could always be relied upon, but success in the play-offs required a veteran presence. Then an incident in Montreal on December 2, 1995, changed the course of the Avalanche's inaugural season.

In a game between the Montreal Canadiens and the Detroit Red Wings, goaltender Patrick Roy was having a particularly difficult night, letting in nine goals and all the while being mocked by the Montreal crowd. Montreal head coach Mario Tremblay and Roy had never liked each other as each tried to assert his dominance in the team. To prove to his player that he was the boss, Tremblay refused to take Roy out of the nets, but finally after the ninth goal, Roy was merci-fully pulled. Roy walked by his coach on the bench, sat down then got up and walked over to the Cana-diens president and told him he had just played his last game as a Montreal Canadien. The Canadiens' loss was the Avalanche's gain, as just four days after the incident, Roy was traded to the Avalanche along with Mike Keane in exchange for Thibault, Martin Rucinsky and Andrei Kovalenko. Although the Avalanche had lost three young players, in return they acquired the missing piece of the puzzle they needed to go far in the playoffs.

With Patrick Roy on the team, the Avalanche suddenly became a contender overnight. Roy played up to his usual standards of excellence and led the Avalanche to a second-place finish overall with 104 total points. Then came the playoffs. The Avalanche made it past the Vancouver Canucks and the Chicago Blackhawks in the first two rounds, but their biggest test came in the Conference finals against the league-leading Detroit Red Wings.

The Draper Incident

By the time the Colorado Avalanche met the Detroit Red Wings in the Conference finals of the 1996 Stanley Cup playoffs, there was already a deeply ingrained hatred between the two clubs. As the two top teams in the Western Conference, they had met many times during the season and over time had built up a natural animosity for each other. But the regular season fisticuffs paled in comparison to the bloodshed that was to come.

Each game was hard fought and filled with violent checking and hatchet stick work, as neither team wanted to give up an inch into their territory. However, after five games, the Avalanche came out on top and led the series by three games to two. Detroit had to win the sixth game if they wanted to remain in the hunt for the Stanley Cup. With everything on the line, the Red Wings were sure to come out hard in the game and battle through each period.

The Avalanche were the first to score, but it was an incident in the first period that would come to define the series and solidify the hatred between the two teams. The incident in question occurred when Red Wings forward Kris Draper stick-handled the puck along the boards in front of the Colorado bench with his back to the ice. At that moment, Avalanche forward Claude Lemieux hit Draper from behind, sending him into the boards face first and causing him to suffer a broken jaw, nose and cheekbone and a severe concussion. Draper would not return to regular play until the middle of the 1996–97 season. Lemieux was given a five-minute major penalty and a game misconduct for the hit. The Avalanche finished the game with a 4–1 win, and Lemieux came out of the dressing room to shake the hands of the Red Wings as is the tradition in playoff hockey. Former Red Wings Dino Ciccarelli said of Lemieux after the game, with no attempt to hide his disgust, "I can't believe I shook the guy's freaking hand. It pisses me off."

What had been an intense rivalry between two competitive teams escalated into full-out hatred over the next few years, and it would erupt into some of the most memorable brawls in hockey.

The First Stanley Cup

After the Avalanche made it out of their bloody Conference final with the Detroit Red Wings, they had nearly a week to rest before battling it out with the Florida Panthers for the Stanley Cup.

Just three seasons prior to the 1996 playoffs, the Florida Panthers and the Colorado Avalanche were not even part of the league, and in that short amount of time they had made it into the Stanley Cup finals. In hockey history, such quick accomplishments by relatively new teams are rare, and every player on both teams knew that this might be the only chance in their careers at lifting the Cup.

Not everyone was surprised to see the Avalanche in position to win the championship with players like Patrick Roy and Joe Sakic, but having the Florida Panthers in the final did not seem likely. The Panthers had finished with a respectable 92 points in the regular season, but the team didn't have the same pedigree of players as the Avs. The Panthers had such hard-nosed veterans as Brian Skrudland, Dave Lowry and goaltender John Vanbiesbrouck, and although Scott Mellanby led the team with a respectable 32 goals, the team looked old and slow compared with the Avs roster.

Realizing that the offensive shortcomings of his team were greater than most, the Panthers head coach had employed a defensive trap technique that made the games boring to watch but gave the Panthers a better chance of winning games. The Panthers had scored 254 goals during the season while the Avalanche had netted 326.

Despite their lack of goal production, the Panthers were one of the best teams at shutting down an opponent's offense. In the Conference finals series against the highest scoring team in the league, the Pittsburgh Penguins, the Panthers had shut down the likes of Mario Lemieux and Jaromir Jagr and defeated them in seven games, never having allowed them more than three goals in one game. The Avalanche knew they were not in for an easy series, given the Panthers habit of surprising during the year, but they were confident that they had enough firepower and skill in net to break the Panthers' system.

Game one at the McNichols Sports Arena started off in favor of the Panthers when Tom Fitzgerald scored in the first period, but three straight unanswered goals by the Avalanche and 25 saves by Patrick Roy sealed the opening win for the home team.

Game two was a nightmare for the Panthers. In just one game, the Avalanche had seemingly figured out the Panthers' defensive system and how to find all the holes in their game. Peter Forsberg opened up the floodgates early in the game with an unassisted goal at 4:41 of the first period. He scored two more goals as his team went on to destroy the Panthers by a final score of 8–1.

The defeat was a bitter pill for the Panthers to swallow, and they hoped a return to their home arena would get them back in the series. But the

Avalanche came away with a 3–2 win and a three-games-to-none advantage in the series. With nothing else to lose in game four, the Panthers tightened up on defense even more, and by the end of the third period, neither team had scored a goal. Fans knew that they were in for a marathon game, and by the start of the third overtime period, no one had yet scored a goal. It was like watching the two coaches play a very long defensive game of chess as neither wanted to give up any ground. But someone had to score eventually, and that honor was given to Avalanche defenseman Uwe Krupp when a seemingly harmless shot from the blueline drifted through the crowd of players in front of the Panther net and found itself behind the goaltender. The Avalanche players flew off the bench and onto the ice, swarming their hero of the moment.

Although Patrick Roy could have easily earned the Conn Smythe Trophy for his outstanding play in the post season, Joe Sakic led all skaters, with 18 goals and 34 points, and took home the honor instead. The Avalanche raised the first Stanley Cup banner in the Mile High City, a moment that will never be forgotten.

The 1996 Stanley Cup victory also created numerous firsts and major personal achievements for several Avalanche players. The Avalanche became the first NHL team to win a championship the first year after relocation and only the second American major sports franchise to accomplish the same feat

(Washington Redskins did it in 1937). Furthermore, winning the Cup made the Avalanche the first Colorado team to win a major professional title. The Denver Spurs' 1971–72 WHL title was the only other professional championship won in the state. Individually, Russians Alexei Gusarov and Valeri Kamensky and Swede Peter Forsberg earned the final leg necessary to join the International Ice Hockey Federation's Triple Gold Club, an elite group of players who have won Olympic Gold, World Championship Gold and the Stanley Cup in their career.

The Brawl in Hockeytown

For the Detroit Red Wings, it was like rubbing salt in their wounds. Not only did the Avalanche defeat the Red Wings in the Conference finals and smash the face of one of their teammates, but they went on to win the Stanley Cup as well. Over the summer, the Red Wings had time to think of the playoff loss, of the insulting injury to one of their most respected players and of having watched Claude Lemieux raise the Cup over his head. Sports pundits were already talking about when the two teams would meet again the following season. The Red Wings had a score to settle with the Avalanche and especially Claude Lemieux.

Surprisingly, when the two teams met up for the first time in the 1996–97 season, nothing out of the ordinary occurred. They played each other two more times without incident, but then on the night of

HOCKEY   53

March 26, 1997, all hell broke loose. Claude Lemieux had not dressed for any of the three earlier games, which was a main reason that no fights had broken out. However, in the fourth game against the Red Wings, Lemieux was thrown into the lineup. Tensions were clearly evident in the first period as Avalanche defenseman Brent Severyn and Wings defenseman Jamie Pushor started the night off with a fight before the five-minute mark. It was then followed by another fight between the Wings Kirk Maltby and Avalanche René Corbet at the 10-minute mark.

With a few minutes left in the first period, the Red Wings seized their chance to get back at Lemieux. During a scrum after a collision at mid-ice between the Avs Peter Forsberg and Wings Igor Larionov, Red Wings tough guy Darren McCarty took advantage of the distracted linesmen trying to break up the melee and took a swing at Lemieux, hitting him with a right hook on the side of his face. McCarty managed to get in a few more blows before Lemieux fell to the ice to protect himself. McCarty hit Lemieux a couple more times, dragging him along the ice and even giving him a knee to the head before officials separated the two.

It was while McCarty was raining fists down on Lemieux that Avs goaltender Patrick Roy skated out to help his teammate but was intercepted with an open ice body check by Red Wings forward Brendan Shanahan. The check sent both players flying through the air. Avs defenseman Adam Foote immediately came to his goaltender's defense and began to tussle with Shanahan. Wings goaltender Mike Vernon then raced in to help Shanahan and found himself in a fight at center ice with Patrick Roy that ended in both goaltenders bleeding from cuts to the face. Eventually the officials got control of the game and handed out penalties to both teams. The brawl left large patches of blood on the ice, which the Zamboni had to clean up.

Officials had hoped that the two teams had settled their differences, but just 15 seconds after play resumed, the Avs Adam Deadmarsh and Wings Vladimir Konstantinov dropped their gloves for another fight. Before the final whistle blew, there would be five more fights. The Red Wings ended up winning the brawl in hockeytown by a final score of 6–5 in overtime on a Darren McCarty goal.

After the game, McCarty commented on the fights. "Guys just got paired off. I guess it was just God's will I got paired off with Lemieux," he said. "Forsberg started the whole thing. But that's the way hockey is. Sometimes things like that happen when you're seven years old and you have to wait until you're 10 to get back at the guy. Some guys are still getting even for things that happened when they were kids. You just wait for your chances. It was intense."

Avs defenseman Adam Foote commented on his goaltender's fight. "You've got to have a lot of respect for Patrick, getting into it, a guy like that. He didn't have to do something like that," he said.

Bad Blood Continued

Despite getting the frustrations out of their system in that March game, the bad blood between the two teams further escalated throughout the Conference finals when another all-out brawl erupted on the ice. While officials on the ice were breaking up the fights, Avs head coach Marc Crawford climbed up onto the glass that separates the two benches and screamed his opinions down upon Red Wings coach Scotty Bowman.

The Red Wings finally got their chance to air their original gripe against Claude Lemieux during a November game of the 1997–98 season. At the opening face off, Red Wings enforcer Darren McCarty lined up beside the Avs Claude Lemieux and the two began to trade punches the moment the puck was dropped. The fight ended in a draw, and presumably the bad blood had been wiped clean. However, on April 1, 1998, when the two teams squared off near the end of the season, another melee broke out at center ice. Patrick Roy skated into the mix and challenged Wings goaltender Chris Osgood to a fight. The officials tried to keep the two apart, but Roy was determined to get at his target. Osgood and Roy then began trading punches at center ice. Fans watching the game at home will remember the announcer screaming with violent delight as Roy pounded Osgood. With each punch, the announcer screamed, "Another right by Roy! Another right! Uppercut! Yeah! You better believe it, baby!"

There was another incident in March 2002 when a mini brawl broke out between Patrick Roy and Red Wings goaltender Dominik Hasek, but the referees stopped the fight.

Since those days, the hatred between the two teams has died down to quiet resentment. However, the history is there, and all it would take is another minor incident to reignite the passions once again.

Mission 16W and the Second Cup

Boston Bruins defenseman Ray Bourque came to a gut-wrenching decision during the 1999–2000 NHL season. The Bruin great, and arguably one of the best defensemen ever, played 21 years on the Boston blueline without tasting a Stanley Cup victory—regardless of his team competing in 19 playoff seasons. Bourque came close on several occasions, winning almost every other award an individual could obtain in the sport, but he never won the game's ultimate prize.

Facing the possibility of becoming one of the greatest players in history without a championship under his belt, Bourque requested a trade mid-season, and the Bruins organization obliged him with a trade to the Colorado Avalanche a week before the trade deadline. To obtain the services of the five-time Norris Trophy winner and 19-time NHL All-Star, along with veteran Dave Andreychuk, the Avs sent Brian Rolston, Samuel Pahlsson, Martin Grenier and a first-round pick back east to Boston.

HOCKEY 57

At the time, Bruins general manager Harry Sinden prophetically quipped these famous words to Bourque, "This may not be your first choice, but this is the team I feel is best."

Bourque joined an Avalanche team positioned well in the Western Conference and poised to make good on Sinden's words. Colorado finished first in the Northwest Division and cruised through the first two rounds of the playoffs, quickly disposing of the Phoenix Coyotes and bitter-enemy Detroit Red Wings 4–1 in both series. Meanwhile, the Dallas Stars were enjoying a similarly easy path to the Conference Finals by eliminating the Edmonton Oilers and San Jose Sharks in the process. For the second year in a row, Colorado and Dallas were pitted against each other in the Western Conference finals, and again Dallas reigned as champions of the West. The Avalanche were denied their chance at a second NHL title, while Bourque, verging on age 40, still pined for his first.

In the off-season, Bourque bypassed retirement and re-signed with the Colorado Avalanche for one more season. The 2000–01 campaign was dubbed "Mission 16W," referring to the 16 playoff-wins requisite to obtain the Stanley Cup. Garrisoned by the likes of Peter Forsberg, Joe Sakic and Patrick Roy, Bourque was playing on possibly the greatest team of his career. In the regular season, the Avs won the President's Trophy as the league's top team with 118 points (a 52–16–10 record), a tally bested by only five other teams ever. The team easily captured yet another Northwest Division championship and swept away the Vancouver Canucks in the playoffs' first round.

The Los Angeles Kings awaited, and as it turned out, provided the Avs their most difficult test all season in more ways than one. Colorado choked away a 3–1 series lead, being shutout in the next two games and forced to win a game seven to advance to the Cup finals. The Avs enjoyed an easy victory, 5–1 over the Kings, but it came at a cost. Star center Peter Forsberg was lost for the rest of the playoffs after having his spleen removed.

The next series proved much less eventful as it took Colorado just five games to move past the St. Louis Blues and arrange a meeting with the Eastern Conference champion, the New Jersey Devils. Both teams exchanged punches during the seven-game series, but the Avalanche delivered the last blow in the final game. Colorado took an insurmountable 3–0 lead by the second period, which New Jersey proved unable to equalize. With the victory, the Avs took their second Stanley Cup championship and Ray Bourque realized the one accomplishment that had remained elusive for so many seasons. When asked about Bourque winning his first title following the victory, the now four-time Stanley Cup champion Patrick Roy, remarked, "A name was missing from that [Cup], and today it is back to normal." Bourque retired after the 2000–01 playoff run.

HOCKEY   59

After the Avs won the Stanley Cup, Colorado governor Bill Owens officially declared June 11, 2001, "Colorado Avalanche Day" statewide. Additionally, captain Joe Sakic received a key to the City of Denver.

In honor of Bourque's phenomenal career and Stanley Cup victory, the Avs made him the first player in franchise history to have his jersey retired despite playing only two seasons for Colorado. A ceremony was held in Bourque's honor on November 24, 2001, to retire his number 77; subsequently, the number 33 of Patrick Roy and 19 of Joe Sakic were retired. Wayne Gretzky's number 99 was also retired by the Avalanche as part of a league-wide mandate in 2001.

Another Great Finnish

Jari Kurri's NHL achievements are too lengthy to enumerate for the purposes of this book, but one record remained unclaimed before he joined the Colorado Avalanche. Kurri began his NHL career with the Edmonton Oilers and became a five-time Stanley Cup winner alongside players such as Wayne Gretzky, Mark Messier, Esa Tikkanen, Glenn Anderson, Paul Coffey and Grant Fuhr—an intimidating list to say the least. After the break up of the core of the Oilers, one of the most dynamic franchises in hockey history, Kurri opted to play a year in Italy before joining the Los Angeles Kings in 1991–92. His old linemate from the Oilers, Wayne Gretzky, joined him the following year (during their career together, Kurri assisted on 196 of Gretzky's goals, and Gretzky assisted on 364 of Kurri's goals). The two continued their successful chemistry and helped the franchise reach the Stanley Cup finals in 1992–93. Kurri played one more year with the Kings after the 1994 lockout then bounced around the NHL for a few seasons before signing with the Colorado Avalanche in 1997–98, his final NHL campaign.

Kurri entered the 1997–98 season four goals short of 600 on his record-breaking career. It took 38 games, but on December 23, 1997, with the Avalanche playing against the Kings, Kurri scored his 600th goal to become the eighth player in NHL history to reach that milestone. Kurri would only pot one more tally during the remainder of the season; he retired from the NHL after his one-year stint with the Avalanche. Kurri finished his career as the highest scoring European-born-and-trained player with 1398 points (many of his marks have been passed since). He also finished with 106 career playoff goals and 233 playoff points, third all-time behind former teammates Gretzky and Messier. His number 17 has been retired by the Oilers, by the Finnish National Team and by his former professional team in Finland, Jokerit.

Colorado Hockey Facts

- The last active NHL player to have skated for the Rockies was defenseman Joe Cirella. He began his career with the Rockies in 1981–82 then moved along with the franchise to play for the New Jersey Devils, then the Quebec Nordiques, the New York Rangers, the Florida Panthers and finally retiring as a member of the Ottawa Senators in 1996.

- The Colorado Avalanche (formerly the Quebec Nordiques) and the New Jersey Devils (formerly the Colorado Rockies) met each other in the 2001 Stanley Cup finals with the Avalanche winning the deciding seventh game in Denver.

- The first captain of the Colorado Rockies was Simon Nolet (1976–77), and the final captain was Rob Ramage (1981–82).

- In the entire history of the NHL, only seven players were born in Colorado. Joe Noris was the first, drafted by the Pittsburgh Penguins in 1971 and continuing his NHL career through 1974, followed by Mike Eaves (1978–1985), Parris Duffus in 1997, John Grahame (2000 to 2008), David Hale (2003 to present), B.J. Crombeen (2008 to present) and Ben Bishop in 2009.

- Goaltender John Grahame was a member of the 2003–04 Stanley Cup champion Tampa Bay Lightning, and as is custom, he had his name engraved on the trophy. His mother, Charlotte, also had her name engraved on the

Cup, making them the only mother and son combination to have their names on the Holy Grail of hockey. As a member of the front office for the Colorado Avalanche when they won the Cup in 2001, she had the privilege of having her name go down in hockey history.

- Patrick Roy retired as a member of the Colorado Avalanche with 551 wins. The number ranked first all-time when Roy ended his career in 2003 (Martin Brodeur passed the record on March 17, 2009). Roy also owns or shares a tie for the following playoff records: games played, minutes played, wins and shutouts.
- The Nordiques retired the number 26 of Peter Stastny before moving to Colorado, but the number is now worn by his son, and current Avalanche, Paul Stastny.
- Paul Stastny holds the record for longest point streak by a rookie through a season, with 20 games (February 3, 2007 to March 17, 2007).
- Former Avalanche Sandis Ozolinsh owns the record for most consecutive games played by a defenseman (495). The first 270 games came with the Nashville Predators and the final 225 in an Avalanche uniform.
- Joe Sakic holds the record for most playoff over-time game-winning goals (8).
- The Avalanche franchise holds the record for most consecutive NHL division titles (9) from 1994–95 to 2002–03.

HOCKEY   63

- Former Avalanche player Peter Forsberg passed countryman Markus Naslund on the final day of the 2002–03 NHL season to become the first Swedish player to lead the league in scoring.
- In 2010, Avs blueliner John-Michael Liles set a new NHL record for the longest assist streak by a defenseman to begin a season at nine games. He broke the previous mark of eight consecutive games with an assist set by Ottawa's Filip Kuba in 2008–09.
- On October 6 and 7, 2010, the Colorado Avalanche held a 15-year Stanley Cup anniversary celebration in honor of their victory in 1996. Of the members of that team, only defenseman Adam Foote remains part of the team.
- 1996 Stanley Cup winning forward Adam Deadmarsh's name was misspelled in the engraving process. It read "ADAM DEAD-MARCH." The error was corrected by stamping an "S" over the "C."
- The Pepsi Center opened its doors for business on October 1, 1999. It is currently the home of the Avalanche, the Denver Nuggets and the Colorado Mammoth of the National Lacrosse League.
- The Colorado Avalanche set the NHL record for the longest consecutive attendance sellouts, with 487 days. The streak began on November 9, 1995, on the Avalanche's eighth home game during the 1995–96 regular season, with

an attendance of 16,061 at the McNichols Sports Arena versus the Dallas Stars. Almost 11 years later, it ended on October 16, 2006, after a reported attendance of 17,681, which is 326 under capacity at Pepsi Center, before a game against the Chicago Blackhawks. The Avalanche recorded their 500th home sellout in their 515th game in Denver on January 20, 2007, against the Detroit Red Wings.

Colorado Rockies Records

- Wilf Paiement recorded the most assists (56) and points (87) in the 1977–78 season, as well as most goals (41) in a season, in 1976–77.
- Rob Ramage posted the most penalty minutes in a season (201), in 1981–82.
- Most wins in a season (16) was by goalie Glenn "Chico" Resch, in 1981–82.

Colorado Hockey Quotes

"That was one of the best groups I've ever been around. We were so close on and off the ice."

–Joe Sakic, on the 1996 Stanley Cup winning team

"We knew we had a great shot at winning and we overlooked all the small problems that we might have faced. History will tell, but for me it was the most talented hockey team I ever played with."

–Claude Lemieux, on the 1996 Stanley Cup winning team

HOCKEY   65

• Background: The Chicago Blackhawks were playing the Colorado Avalanche in the 1996 playoffs when Jeremy Roenick got loose on a breakaway and was hauled down before getting to Patrick Roy's net. Roenick later told the media, "There should have been a penalty shot (on the play). I like Patrick's comment when he said he could have stopped me. I'd like to know where Patrick was in Game 3, probably trying to get his jock out of the rafters."

To which Patrick Roy replied with his now famous line: "I can't really hear what Jeremy says because I've got my two Stanley Cup rings plugging my ear(s)."

"He punched me. If that's his best punch, he'll be in trouble some day."

–Patrick Roy, after his 1997 fight with Red Wings goaltender Mike Vernon

Chapter Three

Baseball

A Long-standing Relationship

For most fans, Colorado baseball begins and ends with the Rockies and their brief existence in Major League Baseball (MLB). But long before 1993 (when the Rockies began), professional baseball occupied the hearts and minds of Coloradoans. Over a century before the Rockies' inception, the Denver Mountain Lions played professional ball in the Western League. The Mountain Lions gave way to the Grizzlies until the team ceased operations in 1891 then returned 10 years later.

Professional baseball's rich tradition in Colorado (principally Denver) has not wavered since that point, except for a few years in which a team did not take the field. Other Colorado municipalities (Colorado Springs, Trinidad, Pueblo, Cañon City, La Junta and Leadville) laid claim to baseball long before Major League Baseball moved to town. Teams like the Pueblo Bighorns, Leadville Blues and Cañon City/Raton Swastikas, and every other club in between, deserve credit for building a passionate fervor for baseball in the Centennial State for nearly 100 years. In all, more than 20 professional baseball teams called Colorado home before 1993, even in places such as Aspen and Breckenridge.

Meet Me in New York

Many are familiar with Billy Martin for his notorious Yankee days; they were rife with infamous tirades and dirt-filled interactions with umpires and they included a tempestuous relationship with owner George Steinbrenner and being hired and fired five times. Martin's managerial career wasn't completely negative, as he won the 1977 World Series during his first stint as Yankees manager. What is little known is that Martin's coaching career actually began in Denver where he obtained his first managerial gig with the 1968 Denver Bears, then the AAA affiliate of the Minnesota Twins in the Pacific Coast League. Martin inherited a 7–22 team in May that he turned into a winning team (73–72) by season's end. It was also in Denver that Martin first coached the great third baseman Graig Nettles. In 1968, Nettles was a standout slugger for the Bears, hitting .297 with 22 home runs and 83 RBIs. Initially, Nettles didn't appreciate the abrasive and sometimes caustic managerial style presented by Martin, but he later attributed his mental and physical toughness to his longtime manager.

Nettles ascended to the big leagues by 1968, joining the Minnesota Twins, but was traded to Cleveland in 1970 before playing three seasons with the Indians. The New York Yankees landed Nettles via a trade in 1973, and two years later he was reacquainted with his old skipper from the Denver Bears (and the Twins after the Bears), Billy Martin. Martin also took a circuitous route through Minnesota, Detroit and Texas prior to joining the Yankees in 1975. Martin was able to turn around a struggling Yankee ballclub and eventually reached baseball's highest peak, the World Series championship, in 1977—an accomplishment owed in large part to Nettles' best season as a professional: 37 home runs, 107 RBIs and the Gold Glove at third base.

Undoubtedly, the Yankees of the late 1970s under Martin were successful in the standings, but the team also created a sideshow vis-à-vis the players' antics and run-ins with each other in the dugout and clubhouse. In regard to this point, Nettles said, "When I was a little boy, I wanted to be a baseball player and join a circus. With the Yankees I've accomplished both."

Record-setting Attendance

Considered one of Minor League Baseball's all-time great franchises, the Denver Bears are firmly vested in history, particularly for astonishing attendance marks. The Bears franchise originally played at Merchant's Park, located at Exposition and Broadway on the city's south side, until it gave way to the new 16,000-seat Bears Stadium in 1948.

By 1963, Bears Stadium had expanded to 25,000 seats as rising attendance figures necessitated the growth. The arrival of the Denver Broncos in 1960 initiated even more change for Bears Stadium—specifically a name change to Denver Mile High Stadium in 1968 because many thought it was inappropriate for a professional football team to play in a stadium donning a minor league baseball team's name. Additionally, a stipulation of the NFL-AFL merger required a minimum 50,000-seat stadium for each of its franchises, and through other additions, Mile High burgeoned to a 76,000-seat capacity by 1977.

Each of these developments provided the Denver Bears with the opportunity to draw throngs of fans, who annually led Minor League Baseball in attendance figures. The biggest crowd each year came on the Fourth of July as fans flocked to see the Bears' impressive fireworks show following the game. One particular celebration, on July 4, 1982, drew 65,666 to Mile High Stadium—the all-time record for attendance at a single Minor League Baseball game!

Number 37

Bears fans came out in droves not just for the atmosphere and experience but also to see a talented team take the field every night, especially throughout the 1970s and 1980s. In a special report delivered by Minor League Baseball, the 1980 Denver Bears were named the "No. 37 Best Minor League Baseball Team" of the 20th century. That Bears team led the Western Division standings for all but the first eight days of the season, finishing a staggering 21½ games better than second-place Oklahoma City. The Bears' final record of 92–44 (.676) came as a result of talented individuals like future MLB Hall of Famer Tim Raines, who won the American Association batting title (.354), set a new league stolen base record (77) and tied for the league lead in triples (11). Raines' teammate, DH Randy Bass, led the league in home runs (37) and RBIs (143) along with runs scored (106) and slugging percentage (.644).

By season's end, the Bears' dominance was clear, finishing atop the American Association in eight major categories, including batting average, runs, hits and home runs, among others. Similarly impressive, the Bears boasted four of the nine hitters in the American Association with a .300 average during the 1980 season. The Bears weren't just adept at hitting; they could pitch as well, ending the season with 14 shutouts and the league's second-ranked earned run average (.387), just behind the .386 mark set by Springfield. Pitchers Bill Gullickson and Steve Ratzer led a Bears team filled with seven all-stars and 24 future major leaguers into the playoffs against Eastern Division champions, Springfield. Regrettably, the Bears' phenomenal regular season had no bearing on their postseason performance, as they lost to the Redbirds four games to one.

The Colorado Connection

One of baseball's finest pitching accomplishments, the no-hitter, rarely occurs in the regular season, let alone the postseason when stakes are the highest. Only two pitchers in the history of MLB have thrown no-hitters in the postseason, and Colorado can lay claim to both: Don Larsen (a one-time Denver Bear) and Roy Halladay (a native Coloradoan).

As a member of the New York Yankees organization in 1955, Don Larsen played a partial season for the team's minor league affiliate Denver Bears (Larsen especially loves to extol the 10 home runs he hit that year in Denver). His stint in Denver was short-lived because of a "call-up" from the Yankees. A year later, Larsen's life and the game of baseball changed forever.

The fifth game of the 1956 World Series saw the New York Yankees and their inner-city rivals, the Brooklyn Dodgers, knotted in a 2–2 series deadlock. The Yankees tapped the 26-year-old Larsen to start game five and hopefully gain a critical 3–2 hold on the series. Larsen's regular season statistics were solid, posting an 11–6 record and 3.26 ERA, but this was his first postseason appearance in 1956. A year earlier he lost the only other playoff game (a World Series game) he ever pitched. On October 8, 1956, in front of 64,519 fans at Yankee Stadium, Larsen retired all 27 hitters he faced (including stars such as Jackie Robinson, Duke Snider, Peewee Reese, Roy Campanella and Gil Hodges) without surrendering a hit or walk. It was the first perfect game ever thrown in major league playoff history. By all accounts, Larsen's outing that evening remains the single greatest postseason pitching performance of all time.

Doc Halladay

Not until the 2010 major league playoffs would another pitcher approach the feat accomplished by Don Larsen, and it took 54 years and 952 postseason games to get there. Philadelphia Phillies' pitcher Roy Halladay, born and raised in Arvada, Colorado, came one batter away from his own perfecto against the Cincinnati Reds in game one of the National League Division Series.

The only blemish on Halladay's scorecard that night was a fifth-inning walk to the Reds' Jay Bruce; otherwise he would have been equally perfect as Larsen. Halladay's playoff "no-no" came on the heels of his thrilling perfect game thrown in the regular season against the Florida Marlins. In fact, Halladay is the only pitcher to throw a perfect game and a no-hitter in the same season.

The Goose

Athletes are often inappropriately described as warriors or heroes, and in the vast majority of cases, these superlatives are empty, misused platitudes. Yet, such descriptions of Colorado's native son, Richard Michael "Goose" Gossage, seem only fitting. Of the 85 Coloradoans to make the major league ranks, Gossage remains the most prestigious.

The man dubbed Goose by former White Sox teammate Tom Bradley for the way he craned his neck to receive a catcher's signal blazed a new trail for pitchers as he defined the relatively new closer's role over a 22-year career—playing for nine different teams. Gossage wielded a one-pitch arsenal consisting of an electric fastball that regularly clocked 98 to 102 miles per hour. But what set the Goose apart was his unwavering durability and no-nonsense approach as he championed the multiple-out and multi-inning save throughout his career. Gossage says of his pitching style, "I was so aggressive on the mound and thought I could throw the ball by anyone. I was so high up there in terms of how I went about my job and being overpowering."

For his career accomplishments, the MLB Hall of Fame came calling on Gossage and he finally entered Cooperstown in 2008, 14 years after retiring from baseball. It took a total of nine attempts for him to finally be elected.

Sterling Statistics

Gossage's final career numbers were astonishing and still rank him among the game's best relief pitchers: 310 saves, 1002 games pitched, 115 wins and

1502 strikeouts. To this day, Gossage still holds the New York Yankees' career record for ERA (2.14) and hits per nine innings (6.59). He led the American League in saves three times and was voted to the All-Star Team on nine occasions. The true measure of Gossage's greatness came in his ability to pitch multiple innings with unrivaled success. Gossage recorded a total of 193 "long-saves"; in other words, saves that required more than three outs. He ranks first all-time in that category ahead of names that are often given more praise and credence than Gossage: Bruce Sutter (188), Mariano Rivera (98) and Trevor Hoffman (55).

More impressively, Gossage earned 24 saves that required nine-plus outs and 101 saves of six-to-eight outs—a feat that will never again be accomplished in baseball, given the less demanding nature of the position in today's game. The present-day closer is typically never asked to pitch more than three outs, with four- and five-out saves coming on rare occasions. Undoubtedly, far more was required of Gossage when his managers brought him into a ball game than any other relief pitcher in history.

In the years following his retirement and induction into baseball's most prestigious fraternity, Gossage has been very outspoken about his accomplishments and the constitution of today's closers. Gossage is not ashamed to say that his merits in the role were far greater than today's best: "They say Mariano Rivera is the greatest pitcher of all time, and

I say, 'Do what we did and we'll compare apples to apples instead of apples to oranges'. It's not the same position."

No matter how many comparisons are made between the game's former and current closers, nobody can deny Gossage's Hall of Fame worthiness, to which he said, "I can't even really comprehend my career. Really, I just can't believe that a kid from Colorado, just a big fan of the game—it's totally overwhelming being elected to the Hall and to have had the career that I did."

The Origins of the Rockies

Having the major league bring its brand of American baseball to the great state of Colorado and having it centered in Denver had always seemed like a winning proposition, but for many years before the Colorado Rockies arrived, professional baseball in the Mile High City was a distant dream.

One of the main efforts to get baseball to Colorado first came in the late 1970s when the Oakland Athletics ran into financial difficulties, in large part because they lacked support. The Athletics had scraped the bottom of the league through most of the 1970s, and by 1978, owner Charles Finley began looking for ways to move his team out of California. Attendance had dropped so low that fans dubbed the Oakland Coliseum the "Oakland Mausoleum."

There was just one issue barring Finley from packing up the team and moving to another city—

Oakland would not allow the team to break its 10-year lease with the coliseum. The entire deal to move the team to Denver rested on breaking this contract, but Oakland held firm. For several months in 1978, baseball fans in Denver had to watch and wait while a series of closed-door meetings determined the fate of major league baseball in their city. Even MLB commissioner Bowie Kuhn got involved in the contract talks with Oakland to help facilitate the move to Denver, but in the end, Oakland refused to break the contract.

In the early 1980s, there was renewed hope of getting a professional team in Denver when the league considered a new round of expansions, but again the Mile High City was left without. This time, instead of contract issues, baseball in Denver was halted by snow.

In October 1984, the Denver Broncos played the Green Bay Packers on Mile High Stadium's open-air field, a game televised before a national audience. The air was unusually cold that day, and by the time of the opening kickoff, a full-scale blizzard descended upon the field. Playing in cold, sometimes snowy conditions was nothing new for Denver or Green Bay, but for the fans watching the game on TV, the image of Denver as a place for all sports was severely damaged.

Then-mayor Federico Peña, a major supporter of bringing professional baseball to Denver, said that the blizzard had hurt the city's image and its ability to attract major league baseball. "It was distressing...a very unfortunate set of circumstances," said the mayor. In his estimation, Denver had been unfairly saddled with the image of being a winter playground for skiers and hockey players, and as a city in the mountains, unsuitable for America's pastime. It was an image the city could not shake, and Denver again got overlooked when new cities were considered for MLB expansion.

But baseball fans in Denver never gave up the dream, and in the early 1990s a renewed hope for the arrival of baseball sprung up once more, led by Larry Varnell of the Colorado Baseball Commission. As the league considered expanding to new cities across the U.S., the only remaining obstacle for Denver baseball was finding a suitable facility to support a pro team. Mile High Stadium had begun to show its age and was not equipped to provide the luxury boxes and VIP seats that the new team needed.

Building a modern baseball field with a seating capacity of over 50,000 is a costly venture, in the realm of $300 million. Securing private funding for the total amount was impossible. Then Varnell came up with the idea of a 0.1 percent sales tax increase that would be used to fund the new stadium. The proposal was put to a vote among Denver's population and they agreed. With the stadium obstacle out of the way, after decades of trying to bring the MLB to Denver, the league finally approved the creation of a new franchise in 1991 that would compete at the start of the 1993 season.

The Colorado Rockies played their first game on April 5, 1993, against the New York Mets at Shea Stadium with David Nied pitching in a 3–0 loss. The franchise's first home game at Mile High Stadium came just four days later in an 11–4 win over the Montreal Expos. The team's first win was viewed by more than 80,000 baseball-hungry fans, to date the largest crowd to see a single regular-season MLB game.

The Mile High Asterisk

Since their creation in 1993, the achievements of the Colorado Rockies seemed to have more asterisks attached to their name than Barry Bonds' career. This is because playing one mile, or 5280 feet, above sea level in the thinner atmosphere does certain things to the human body and to the physics of baseball that lead to some advantages and other disadvantages as well.

In high altitude, two different types of effects come into play when considering the ability of athletes to play their sport. One is physiological, determined by the body's reaction to a thin, less oxygen-rich atmosphere. The second speaks to the specific sport itself and how it is altered by performing in the high altitude.

When a human body is exposed to high altitudes and a reduced atmospheric environment, a built-in mechanism is triggered to counteract the effect of the low oxygen level.

The body senses that it is not receiving the required amount of oxygen and begins to produce a greater number of red blood cells to carry oxygen into the blood stream. This increase in red blood cell oxygen transportation ensures that the available oxygen is optimized.

Athletes who are accustomed to high altitudes will have a direct advantage over their competitors, as the increased oxygen to their bodies is a proven, effective performance-enhancing tool. The effects of high altitude on athlete performance were brought to wide attention during the 1968 Olympics in Mexico City, which sits 7349 feet above sea level. American Bob Beamon set a new long jump record at 29 feet 2 inches, which shattered the old record by two feet in a sport where records are broken in fractions of inches. At 5500 feet above sea level, Colorado sports franchises enjoy a natural advantage over their visiting teams, particularly when it comes to baseball.

High-altitude Stats

Although the Colorado Rockies no longer play at the aptly named Mile High Stadium, their current home at Coors Field still sits one mile above sea level, making players susceptible to the effects of the high altitude. Because of the increase in oxygen in the body, those who were accustomed to playing in that environment were in a sense stronger than their opposition, and as a result, the production of home runs increased.

This increase in home runs can be seen in the statistics of former Colorado Rockies outfielder Larry Walker. Always known as a power hitter when he started out with the Montreal Expos, Walker's home-run stats nearly doubled when he was traded to the Rockies in 1995. He went from hitting a high of 23 home runs while with the Montreal Expos (Montreal sits at an altitude of 153 feet above sea level) to a career-high 49 home runs in 1997 with the Rockies.

The higher altitude also affects the game itself. Research has shown that a baseball will travel between three percent and seven percent farther through the Denver atmosphere than a similarly struck ball at sea level. The distance a pitched ball has to travel is too short to measure any effects from the high altitude.

Scientifically this all makes sense; however, science still can't explain why the Rockies have not won the World Series.

Humidor Controversy

As records continued to fall at alarming rates at Coors Field, Rockies management decided to introduce an innovative, yet controversial solution. In 2002, they began to store game balls in a humidor in order to counteract and combat the paper-thin air and inflated statistics of Coors Field.

The humidor was the brainchild of team engineer Tony Cowell, who noticed that his leather hunting boots became tighter and shrank over the summer—precisely what happens to a leather baseball in the dry, hot summer air of Denver. A dry baseball is difficult for pitchers to grip and because of its higher density, it travels farther, which is exponentially more dangerous when combined with high-altitude air. Tests revealed that baseballs at high altitude were lighter and slicker than those used around the MLB, which was another challenge incurred by Rockies' pitchers already trying to combat the extra distance a baseball travels in the thin air.

The solution was to store their baseballs in a humidor. The humidor works akin to its cigar counterpart by maintaining a consistent level of humidity to prevent the baseballs from drying and compressing. The apparatus is always kept at 70° F and 50 percent humidity in order to keep the baseballs between 5 and 5 1/4 ounces in weight and 9 and 9 1/4 inches in circumference, according to the specification of Rawlings, the official manufacturer of major league baseballs. The miniature, environment-controlled room is roughly 9 feet by 9 wide and 7 feet high and is capable of housing 400 baseballs. A computer controls the precise temperature and humidity levels of the water coils in the humidor.

When Rockies' staff receive a shipment of baseballs, they immediately give them a time and date stamp before moving them to the humidor. Staff also retains a "test" batch of balls pulled from each of the boxes. These balls are constantly tested and measured to provide feedback regarding the efficacy of the humidor, the results of which are reported to Major League Baseball. The baseballs to be used in games are removed from the humidor in the order they have arrived—the first ones in are the first ones out. On game day, 10 to 12 dozen baseballs are removed from the humidor, treated with Mississippi mud, placed back in the humidor and then given to the umpires before first pitch. All unused balls are returned for storage in the humidor to be used at a later date.

It didn't take long for the humidor to create a lasting mark on the brand of baseball played in Denver. In the pre-humidor days, Coors Field averaged a league-high 13.8 runs and 3.2 home runs per game from 1995 to 2001. In 2002, the humidor's first year of service, runs per game fell by more than one to 12.21, and home runs dipped to just 2.8. The numbers continued to drop thereafter, and in Colorado's World Series year of 2007, Coors Field surrendered 10.58 runs and 2.23 home runs per game—a huge difference from the drier, denser days before the humidor. Rockies reliever Todd Jones summed up the benefit of the new apparatus: "It really made a difference. The balls didn't dry out, they weren't as slick. The humidor made them more tacky. At Coors Field, where hitters have an advantage, it made things more even."

Although the new technology is successful in normalizing offensive numbers, the humidor still faces scrutiny from Rockies' opponents and pundits alike.

The most recent complaint came in 2010 when the San Francisco Giants accused the Rockies of slipping "juiced" baseballs into the hands of Giants' pitchers. The Giants alleged that their hometown TV cameras showed the Rockies illegally switching baseballs. In 2006, Brewers third baseman Jeff Cirillo told a Milwaukee radio show that he compared a normal baseball with a humidor ball, stating, "It's all spongy, and it's big, and it's water logged. They're illegal baseballs. They are non-flying baseballs." Major League Baseball, which regulates the use of the humidor, has consistently assured teams that there is no foul play involved. The humidor remains in use today, under the watchful eye of the league, but despite strict regulation and its successful track record, it will continue to draw criticism.

Generation R

In 2004, the Rockies' core group of players had been with the team for a few years, and many of them were beginning to turn gray around the temples. When outfielder and fan favorite Larry Walker was traded to the St. Louis Cardinals, it brought about a major shift in the make-up of the club—fresh-off-the-farm rookies replaced the large veteran presence.

Along with Walker, veterans Vinny Castilla and Jeromy Burnitz were lost to free agency, catcher Charles Johnson was traded to the Boston Red Sox and shortstop Royce Clayton parted company with the Rockies. In their place, the club called up reinforcements, including third baseman Garrett Atkins, outfielder Matt Holliday, fielder Brad Hawpe, second baseman Clint Barmes and catcher J.D. Closser. Other than Todd Helton and a few other players, the majority of the team in 2004 was under 30 years old, hence the nickname, "Generation R."

Christian Baseball

Colorado is a religious state. The majority of the population hold a belief in God and call themselves good Christian folk. Most people keep these beliefs and the way they live their lives private, but in 2006, a story in *USA Today* surfaced that Christian values had found their way into the locker room of the Colorado Rockies.

In their clubhouse, you will not find any copies of *Playboy* or *Penthouse* or even *Vanity Fair*. The only reading materials provided for the players are newspapers, sports and car magazines and the Bible. Bob Nightengale, a reporter for *USA Today*, described the scene in the locker room in his May 2006 article: "Music filled with obscenities, wildly popular with youth today and in many other clubhouses, is not played. A player will curse occasionally but usually in hushed tones. Quotes from Scripture are posted in the weight room. Chapel service is packed on Sundays. Prayer and fellowship groups each Tuesday are well attended. It's not unusual for the front office executives to pray together."

BASEBALL   85

On the field, it was business as usual for the team, but behind the scenes, they were a club that embraced a Christian-based code of conduct that they hoped would bring them success on game day. Rockies general manager Dan O'Dowd explained the team philosophy as a top-down approach, but the club was skittish about revealing their way of thinking.

"We're nervous, to be honest with you," he said. "It's the first time we ever talked about these issues publicly. The last thing we want to do is offend anyone because of our beliefs."

The team philosophy developed largely at the request of Rockies chairman and CEO Charlie Monfort after the club was averaging 91 losses per season, beginning in 1999. Monfort became a reborn Christian in 2003 after years of partying and a conviction for drunk driving that made him look for a better way to lead his life. Christian values had saved his life, so he figured they could make a difference to his team on the field as well.

"We started to go after character six or seven years ago, but we didn't follow that like we should have," Monfort said in the article. "I don't want to offend anyone, but I think character-wise we're stronger than anyone in baseball. Christians, and what they've endured, are some of the strongest people in baseball. I believe God sends signs, and we're seeing those."

The club was quick to point out that none of the Christian values were being forced on the players and that the idea was simply to bring a type of harmony to the team off the field so that they could better perform under pressure on the field. The team's philosophy brought about a slight change in 2006 when they lost only 86 games, instead of 95 in 2005, showing skeptics that whether you have a team of Christians or a team full of sinners, without the fundamentals of baseball, you just can't win games. But regardless of the beliefs, the Rockies improved to a 90–73 record in the 2007 season and for the first time since 1995 earned an appearance in the postseason.

Using faith to motivate players is nothing new in sport. Several minor league clubs, particularly in the South, have held Faith Night promotions that featured Christian rock bands and many players in the NFL and NBA regularly hold prayer meetings and prayer circles before games.

Slate.com writer David Plotz writes, "It is no accident that many athletes believe in God's involvement in all aspects of life, including baseball. Athletes want results, and they want to see them when they pray."

Whether faith can bring success on the field or not is left up to the individual to decide, but all in all, a little help from God never hurt. Just ask the 2007 Rockies and see what they say about God and baseball.

The Run to the Series

After finishing in second place in the National League West at the end of the 2007 season, the Colorado Rockies had managed to secure just their

BASEBALL   87

second overall postseason appearance since joining the majors in 1993. Building a new franchise into a winning club is a difficult proposition and, as many teams have found out, the road to success in the postseason can be elusive. The Rockies were certainly not immune to the process, spending 11 consecutive years out of the playoffs. The people of Denver are a patient, loyal lot, willing to stick by their team through tough years, but after so many seasons without a chance of winning the World Series, even the most diehard Rockies fans were staying away from the home games. Average per game attendance went from 47,000 in 1995 (the year of their first appearance in the postseason) to just under 29,000 by 2007.

Nearing the end of the 2007 MLB season, the Rockies did not appear to be a team ready for the playoffs, trailing behind the division leaders by six games, but a late-September burst of energy saw the team pull together in the final 15 games of the season, losing only once. They qualified for the postseason in the wild card spot, but because they were tied with the San Diego Padres, the two teams were forced to play a tiebreaker game to move on into the playoffs.

On October 1, 2007, the two teams faced off in an epic game that needed extra innings for a winner to be declared. Going into the ninth inning, the game was tied at 6–6 and was headed into an edge-of-your seat, all-or-nothing extra innings match. With their entire season coming down to a few innings, the

Rockies saw the postseason slipping away when in the top of the 13th inning, Padres Scott Hairston belted a two-run home run to make the score 8–6. The Rockies were three outs away from a very long off-season.

The Padres put in their ace closer Trevor Hoffman to secure the lead and finish off the Rockies, but after allowing two doubles and a triple, the game was tied up at 8–8. Hoffman then intentionally walked the Rockies Todd Helton, leaving runners on first and third. Up next was Rockies Jamey Carroll, who blasted a deep line drive to the right field, allowing Matt Holliday to tag up at third and make the sprint to the home plate, just beating out the throw home. Home plate umpire Tim McClelland paused on the call for what seemed like an eternity then waved his arms outward and called safe. The Rockies won the game 9–8 and moved into the playoffs.

Or was Holliday out? Jeff Passan of Yahoo! Sports and Mark Kiszla of the *Denver Post* both wrote that Holliday had never touched home plate, but the call stood on the field, and the Rockies were through to their second playoffs in the team's history.

Rocktober, Part I

"Rocktober" is a very fitting term given to the Colorado Rockies' drive for the World Series championship in October 2007. The Rockies had a solid lineup of players, but sports pundits remained skeptical about how far the team could take it in the postseason up against the powerhouses of the Phila-delphia Phillies and the Arizona Diamondbacks. But a look at all the teams in the postseason shows that the Rockies could stand up against the best, or at least provide a challenge and go down fighting hard.

In game one of the Rockies' National League Division best of five series with the Philadelphia Phillies, Rockies ace pitcher Jeff Francis went up against the Phillies top pitcher Cole Hamels. Both aces led the first by retiring the side in order, but the Rockies Todd Helton got the game started with a triple in his first-ever postseason appearance. That triple led a three-run inning that the Rockies carried through to win the game with a 4–2 final score. The Philly hometown fans did not appreciate the underdog Rockies defeating their team at home and hoped that game two might be a different story. But again Colorado's pitching was solid and consistent, and the Rockies' bats opened up with 12 hits and three home runs, taking game two by a score of 10–5.

Game three was back at home on Coors Field, and a 14-minute blackout caused by some computer malfunction didn't stop the Rockies from completing the series before a home crowd. The Rockies and the Phillies remained tied at one all through the game until the eighth inning when the Rockies scored the go ahead run by Jeff Baker. The Rockies closing ace came in and knocked off the Phillies by a final score of 2–1. Television play-by-play announcer Don Orsillo summed up the feelings of the fans and players: "On the ground, right side, Matsui to first and the Colorado Rockies are going to the National League Championship Series for the first time in franchise history! They're going crazy here in Colorado!"

Rocktober, Part II

The Rockies had moved on to the National League Championship Series for the first time in their history, and they would play the Arizona Diamondbacks for the right to be in the World Series. Statistically, the Diamondbacks had the advantage, but that can change in the playoffs, and the Rockies proved that in every inning of the series.

Opening the series in Arizona, the Rockies were unfazed by the less than welcoming crowd. Rockies pitcher Jeff Francis delivered another pitching gem that allowed nine hits, but just one run, while the Diamondbacks contributed five runs. Game two was closer on the score sheet but the Rockies cool-headed reactions at the plate into extra innings resulted in Arizona pitcher José Valverde throwing a fourth ball to Willy Taveras with the bases loaded.

The bases-loaded walk to lose game two seemed to completely remove any life from the Arizona squad in game three. They could not mount any significant attack under the Rockies tight pitching or the timely home runs from Matt Holliday, which helped propel the Rockies to a four-game sweep of the Diamondbacks and a birth in the World Series to face the

BASEBALL   91

Boston Red Sox. Rockies announcer Jeff Kingery of 850 KOA called the final play the best: "Corpas ready, first pitch, check-swing roller...Tulowitzki has it, throws to first...BALL GAME! WORLD SERIES TIME IN COLORADO! He's done it all year! Tulo gunned it over to first. It's a dream that began in the early '90s when the Rockies were awarded the expansion franchise, and now 15 seasons in, they're going to the World Series! This one is a Rockies winner at Coors Field!"

The 2007 World Series

Rocktober continued on into the World Series, and the Rockies and their fans were optimistic for their chances against the Boston Red Sox. The Rockies had won 21 of their last 22 games and had a record-setting eight-day layoff in between while they waited for the Red Sox to dispense of the Cleveland Indians in the American League Championship Series. Rockies fans had hoped that the Red Sox would be tired after a tough seven-game series against the Indians, but the Red Sox arrived back in Boston filled with energy in their game and fire at the end of their bats.

In game one on October 24, 2007, in Boston's Fenway Park, Jeff Francis was on the mound for the Rockies. But this time the team ace could not put a stop to the heavy hitting of the Red Sox's David Ortiz and Dustin Pedroia, and the Rockies lost the game by an embarrassing score of 13–1.

Although game two was a lot closer on the score-board, the results were the same. The Rockies lost another game to the Red Sox to put them into a dangerous deficit in the series. This time it was the Rockies fans who were hoping their team could pull out the needed win at home. That, unfortunately, was not the case as the Red Sox won both game three and four to sweep the World Series.

While the Red Sox became the first team of the 21st century to win two World Series (the other in 2004), the Rockies had the dubious distinction of being just the second team in MLB history to get swept in the final (the other team to suffer that fate was the 1990 Oakland Athletics). Despite losing the series in a sweep, the Rockies were named by the sports premiere magazine *Baseball America* as the 2007 Organization of the Year.

"We knew they were bringing great talent through their farm system, but we certainly didn't expect it to pay off with big-league success so quickly," said Will Lingo, editor of *Baseball America*. "They won with homegrown players, have more talent on the way and have maintained stability in their front office, so they had pretty much everything we look for in an organization."

Three Seven-inning Stretches

On April 17, 2008, the Colorado Rockies landed in San Diego for a regular-season game, just like they had done many times before, but this time things were different.

Padres pitcher Jake Peavy threw out the first pitch at 7:05 PM and held the Rockies off the score sheet. Eventually Peavy tired of pitching and was replaced, but the game had stretched into the ninth and tenth innings and still neither team had earned a run.

Going into the 14th inning, the Rockies finally got on the board, though they did it without really doing much. Rockies batter Brad Hawpe simply drew a bases-loaded walk to put his team up by one. The Rockies thought they had the game sealed up, given that no runs had scored, but the Padres managed to tie it in the bottom of the inning when a bases-loaded single gave the Padres the point they needed to stay alive in the game.

The game went on, and on, and on into the 22nd inning before Troy Tulowitzki's double to bring in Willy Taveras won the Rockies the game, ending the contest at 1:21 AM. Only a handful of the original 25,984 fans remained in their seats for the final score. In total, there were 658 pitches by 15 pitchers from both teams. At one point, a man in the stands caught a foul ball and was heard screaming, "That's it! I'm going home!" The players were also happy to get the game over with.

"It's tough to keep your head into it and put together good at-bats and be into every pitch," Tulowitzki said. "We were talking about how our legs were hurting out there. It's tough to stand on your feet for 22 innings and keep moving."

Rockies manager Clint Hurdle noticed that his players were a little tight after playing for so long. "This was a good game to get outside yourself," Hurdle said. "About the 16th inning, I said, 'Hey, boys, no matter what's in front of us, there's a world of people out there who've got harder rows to hoe than we do. No matter what happens the rest of the night, have some fun with this thing.'"

Blake Street Batting Titles

In 2010, Rockies centerfielder Carlos González hit for a .336 batting average, on his way to being crowned the National League's batting champion. The Venezuelan youngster, known better as "CarGo," captured the Rockies' seventh batting title, an astonishing number considering the organization's short 18-year existence.

Fellow Venezuelan Andrés Galarraga jump-started the Rockies batting barrage in 1993 as he hovered around the magical .400 average mark throughout the season. On the final day of the season, "The Big Cat" posted a .370 average and defeated legendary Padres hitter Tony Gwynn (.358) for the National League batting crown. In the process, Galarraga posted the highest batting average ever by a Hispanic ballplayer, became the first Venezuelan batting champ and also the first player on an expansion team to win the honor. Gwynn, not to be outdone, won the next four batting titles before the Rockies took a stranglehold on the award in the subsequent four years.

Welcome Walker

In 1997, Rockies right fielder, Larry Walker, became the first Canadian-born player to become the league's most valuable player, hitting .366 with 49 home runs, 130 RBIs, 33 stolen bases and 409 total bases (Walker also won the Gold Glove that season for right field, an honor he won seven times in his career.) Unfortunately, Walker's .366 average finished second to Tony Gwynn's .372.

Walker followed his 1997 MVP season with another phenomenal season in 1998, posting a .363 batting average, which earned Walker his first and the Rockies second batting title. One year later, Walker bested his 1998 season, again leading the National League with a .379 batting average; he also led the NL in on-base percentage and slugging percentage. Walker's .379 mark was a remarkable 43 points higher than runner-up Luis Gonzalez (.336) of the Arizona Diamondbacks.

The year 2000 ushered in a new millennium, a new MLB season and the newest Colorado Rockies' batting champion in Todd Helton. That season, the fan favorite delivered a career year (similar to Walker in 1997), leading the major leagues in batting average (.372), runs batted in (147), doubles (59), total bases (405), extra base hits (103), slugging percentage (.698) and OPS (1.162). In doing so, Helton became just the fourth player to lead the National League in both batting average and RBIs in the same season. Amazingly for the Colorado organization, Helton was its third player to win the batting title and fourth overall.

Just in case three consecutive batting crowns didn't satisfy the Rockies' faithful, Helton and Walker ensured the trophy called Denver home for an astonishing fourth-consecutive season. Both Walker and Helton dazzled at Coors Field, tantalizing fans throughout the summer as they simultaneously flirted with hitting .400. The two teammates, hitting third and fourth in the Rockies' lineup, pushed and motivated each other to a combined 269 RBIs, 371 hits, 89 doubles and 88 home runs. But in the end, only one man could win the batting title, and just as he had done in 1998 and 1999, Walker (.350) recaptured the award from his teammate Todd Helton (.336). Regardless of the victor, both Walker and Helton provided one of the most memorable summers in the Rockies' short history.

Continued Dominance

After setting such a standard during the previous four seasons, it seemed inevitable that a Rockies player would be involved in the batting championship discussion every year. And thanks to a stacked lineup and hitting-friendly surroundings, the Rockies

BASEBALL   97

stalked the rest of the league's hitters on a continual basis. In 2002, Larry Walker threatened again, finishing second to the San Francisco Giants' Barry Bonds, then Todd Helton served as runner-up to the St. Louis Cardinals' Albert Pujols in 2003 (the closest batting title race in NL history), and to Bonds in 2004.

In 2006, two new Rockies' batsmen emerged in the form of Garrett Atkins and Matt Holliday, finishing fourth and fifth, respectively. In 2007, Matt Holliday returned the batting championship to Colorado with a .340 batting average—now the sixth for the franchise. Combined with the aforementioned exploits of Carlos Gonzalez in 2010, the Rockies claim individual batting titles in seven of their 18 big-league seasons. In fact, Colorado owns the highest percentage (38 percent) of batting titles compared to seasons played (18) than any other team in Major League Baseball history.

Rockies Baseball Facts

- The team mascot is Dinger, a purple triceratops.
- Although Jackie Robinson's number 42 is the only jersey number to have been retired (league wide, mind you), since Larry Walker's 2004 departure from the team, his number 33 has not been given out to another player.
- As of 2010, the Baseball Hall of Fame has yet to induct a member into its hallowed halls that has played for the Colorado Rockies.

- Larry Walker won the Gold Glove Award (while playing for the Rockies) in 1997, 1998, 1999, 2001 and in 2002 (he also won it with the Montreal Expos in 1992 and 1993).

- The Colorado Rockies are also known by the nicknames "The Rox" and the "Blake Street Bombers."

- Former Rockies first baseman Andrés Galarraga was nicknamed "The Big Cat" for his quickness and flexibility at first base despite his big frame. In 1993, Galarraga flirted with a .400 batting average all season long. He ended the season with an average of .370 (a 127-point increase over his previous year's total). The total was the highest average since Joe DiMaggio batted .381 in 1939.

- The Rockies nearly made the 2010 postseason, but ending the season with a string of 13 losses in the last 14 games pushed them out of contention.

Baseball Quotes

"It was kind of humbling. It's fun with these type games. When you're on the winning side, it's fun. When you're on the losing side, it's terrible."

–Matt Holliday, on losing a tough game

"He's kind of like that sheep dog that keeps showing up in the cartoon…He punches in, punches out,

he doesn't have a whole lot to say. But you look up at
the board and he's got double-digit homers [10], he's
got [63] RBIs. As I've said all year long, he's hit the
ball harder, with more consistency, and made more
hard outs than anybody on this ballclub right now.
Anytime you've got Todd Helton on your ballclub,
that's something."

–Clint Barmes, Rockies shortstop,
on teammate Todd Helton

Chapter Four

Basketball

The Rockets Evolution

The Denver Nuggets' seven consecutive playoff appearances from 2004 to 2009 reversed the struggles of a franchise formerly plagued by lopsided losing seasons, while also increasing awareness of basketball in Denver. Colorado's first taste of any professional sport came in 1948 with the original Denver Nuggets of the National Basketball League (NBL). Not only were the Nuggets Colorado's first professional team, but they were also the first professional basketball team west of the Mississippi. But, after just one season of play, the NBL merged with the Basketball Association of America to form the current National Basketball Association (NBA). The Nuggets played only one season in the NBA before ceasing operations in 1950, leaving Colorado without a pro sports team for another 10 years.

Professional basketball re-emerged in Colorado for the inaugural 1967–68 American Basketball Association (ABA) season as the charter member

Denver Rockets took the court in the city's Auditorium Arena. The "Rockets" name paid homage to the team's owner, Bill Ringsby, who ran the Denver-based "Ringsby Rocket" Trucking Company and provided the solid, reliable ownership credentials ABA officials were seeking. After four winning seasons in eight ABA campaigns, the franchise looked to make wholesale changes in 1975, including adopting the old "Nuggets" brand to avoid confusion with the NBA's Houston Rockets in case Denver jumped leagues in the future.

The newly named Nuggets altered their coaching ranks as well, naming Carl Scheer the franchise's new headman while retaining Scheer's assistant coach from Carolina, the legendary Larry Brown. The position in Denver was just Brown's second coaching gig in his lengthy, Hall of Fame career.

Two short seasons later, extended financial difficulties and the lack of a national television contract doomed the ABA and its member clubs; however, the ABA would transfer four teams to the NBA. The Nuggets were chosen to join the NBA for the 1976–77 season alongside the New Jersey Nets, Indiana Pacers and San Antonio Spurs, and while the other three teams initially struggled in the new league, the Nuggets flourished. Winning became standard practice in Denver as the team posted a 145–101 record over the next three NBA seasons, making the playoffs each of those years and entrenching their status as a legitimate professional basketball franchise.

The Golden Nugget: Alex English

No doubt one of the greatest players ever to don a Nugget uniform, Alex English played in Denver for 10 seasons and left a lasting impression on the club's history. The Indiana Pacers announced their interest in trading English midway through the 1979–80 season, and the Nuggets could hardly believe their luck when the Pacers accepted a straight-up swap for George McGinnis. McGinnis was a good player, but he was aging, and English was still in his prime and was just beginning to show the talent that would make him one of the top point-getters in NBA history. The trade turned out to be a boon for the Nuggets.

The 1980s was a good time to be a Nuggets fan. When the club hired Doug Moe as head coach in 1981, Moe brought with him a new philosophy in basketball that focused on offense first, and players like Alex English thrived in that offensive environment. Throughout the 1980s, the Nuggets often scored well over 100 points per game, and in the 1981–82 season they scored at least 100 points in 136 consecutive games, setting an almost unbreakable NBA record. At the front of this was forward Alex English, who averaged over 28 points per game during his Denver Nuggets years. As well as leading the Nuggets to victory after victory, English was instrumental in taking the Nuggets into the postseason nine years in a row, though never taking them to the championship.

English's point totals began to drop and in 1990 he was traded to the Dallas Mavericks. Although he ended his career with the Mavericks in 1991, his time with the Nuggets will always be remembered for what he accomplished for the team.

In 1992, the club retired his number 2 jersey to the rafters, and English still remains the Nuggets' leading all-time scorer with 21,645 points. The only active player close to English's points is Carmelo Anthony, who currently sits in the 13,000-point range. English remains in the world of the NBA today as an assistant coach with the Toronto Raptors.

Blazing a New Trail

A quick analysis of NBA rosters reveals a youth-dominated league thriving off star players who seemingly get younger and younger every season. Players are becoming millionaires by age 19, all thanks to Spencer Haywood, a man whom many current players are unfamiliar with. It was Haywood in 1970 who challenged the NBA's youth restriction, which stated that a player must finish four years in college before playing in the league. After just two years at the University of Detroit, Haywood elected to play for the Denver Rockets of the ABA after being rejected for not conforming to the NBA's age requirements.

By signing on with the Rockets, Haywood became the first player to leave college early to join the professional ranks. Starring in Denver, Haywood was voted both the ABA's Rookie of the Year and Most Valuable Player for the 1969–70 season—averaging 30.0 points and 19.5 rebounds per game. His compilation of 986 field goals, 1637 rebounds and 19.5 rebounds per game average still stand as ABA records. In just one ABA season, Haywood displayed his ability to play at higher level, but the NBA's age requirement remained an impregnable obstacle.

In an attempt to gain entrance to the NBA, Haywood and the Seattle SuperSonics jointly sued the league in 1970 (*Haywood v. National Basketball Association*), citing anti-trust laws. Appeals advanced the case to the Supreme Court, but before a ruling materialized, the NBA agreed to settle the matter, allowing Haywood to join the Sonics in 1971.

Regardless of his unpopular stature after the legal ordeal, Haywood went on to be named an NBA All-Star four times, an NBA All-First Team member twice and won the 1979–80 NBA Championship with the Los Angeles Lakers. Haywood's defiance created a new path for underclassmen, permitting NBA stardom and riches at an earlier age.

Mr. Big Shot

Chauncey Billups' trade from the Detroit Pistons to the Denver Nuggets in 2008 not only reunited the Denver native with his former club, but it also returned the state's greatest basketball talent. Colorado has never really been recognized as a basketball factory, but Billups' play at Denver's George

Washington High School put him and the state in the basketball consciousness. Billups starred at George Washington, where he was an All-State selection four times and was named Colorado Mr. Basketball three times and Colorado player of the year on two occasions. McDonalds All-American honors followed, but a shoulder injury kept Billups from participating in the showcase event.

Coloradoans rejoiced when Billups opted to keep his talents in state, enrolling at the University of Colorado–Boulder instead of making himself eligible for the NBA draft. Billups played two years for the Buffaloes, in the process averaging 18.5 points per game, while being named to the Big XII Conference First Team and an All-American by *Basketball Times* his sophomore year. His 1997 team earned a number nine seed in the NCAA tournament and went on to win their first tourney game since 1963 with an 80–62 blowout victory over Indiana. North Carolina knocked the Buffs out of the second round that year, sending Billups to the NBA earlier than anyone in Colorado would have liked.

Rick Pitino and the Boston Celtics selected Billups third overall in 1997, but adversity forced the team to trade Billups to Toronto midway through the season. Trades and injuries hampered Billups as he joined four different NBA teams in his initial five years with the league. The young man who wore number 4 because of his admiration for former Pistons guard Joe Dumars, was then signed as a free agent by his boyhood idol, joining Detroit in 2002. Billups settled in as a proven NBA star with the Pistons, earning the nickname "Mr. Big Shot" for his ability to make critical, last-second buckets. The Denver native was a key cog in the Pistons' mini-dynasty, earning NBA Finals MVP honors while leading his team to the 2004 NBA title. His team again appeared in the 2005 NBA Finals but fell just short to the San Antonio Spurs in an epic seven-game battle. A year later, Billups led the Pistons to a franchise record 64–18, but the team failed to make the NBA Finals for the first time in three seasons.

In recognition of his success, Detroit signed Billups to a four-year, $46-million contract extension in 2007, attempting to lock up the star guard for the foreseeable future. Yet, early in the 2008–09 season, the Nuggets acquired Billups (and others) in exchange for Allen Iverson, whose notoriously capricious antics were no longer welcome in Denver's locker room. Besides the 2004 title and MVP in Detroit, Billups also led the Pistons to six-straight Eastern Conference Finals appearances and a 2005 NBA Finals berth while individually being named an NBA All-Star three times. Billups officially returned home on November 7, for his second stint with the Nuggets, in a game against the Dallas Mavericks.

Returning to Denver in 2008, Billups teamed up with established superstar Carmelo Anthony, a combination that resulted in instantaneous success for the Nuggets. The team's 54–28 record matched the previous franchise best set during the 1987–88 season, at the same time attaining back-to-back 50-win seasons for the first time as an organization. By reaching the Western Conference Finals in 2009 (although it resulted in defeat), Billups joined only five other men to appear in seven-straight Conference Finals series over their NBA career. While in a Nuggets jersey, Billups also established a personal-high 39 points in a 2010 game against the Lakers. Billups' return home came to the delight of Denver fans, and although it wasn't said audibly, echoes of "Welcome back, Mr. Big Shot" could be heard everywhere.

Point-producing Powerhouse

Those familiar with the NBA are well aware the Nuggets franchise is noted for its high-flying, run-and-gun offensive approach and its less than stalwart defensive ability. Given this style of play, the Nuggets have consistently found themselves on either end of blowout contests. One such game occurred on November 10, 1990, as the Nuggets were on the wrong end of a 173–143 score at the hands of the Phoenix Suns. The Suns' 173 points tied the Boston Celtics (1959) for the most points scored by a team in a regulation NBA game. By halftime, the Suns had already reached the 100-point plateau, and eight Phoenix players scored in double digits, led by Cedric Ceballos' 32-point effort. Shockingly, the Suns reached 173 points without making one three-point field goal. Orlando Woolridge's 40-point output led the Nuggets in a losing effort.

Almost two decades later, the Nuggets found themselves in a similar-style game on March 16, 2008, against the Seattle Sonics, but on this occasion Denver emerged victorious, scoring the third-most points (168) by one team in a regulation game. The 168 mark also set a Nuggets' franchise record—it was a remarkable 52 points better than the Sonics, which still scored a more than respectable 116 points. Eight Nuggets scored in double digits, and although you might expect one player to produce a huge number of points, Carmelo Anthony's 26 points were the highest for the Nuggets—a true testament to a balanced scoring attack. Rookie standout Kevin Durant paced the Sonics with 23 points.

Not surprisingly, the Denver Nuggets have also found themselves involved in some of the NBA's record-setting overtime match-ups. It took three extra stanzas on December 13, 1983, but the Detroit Pistons defeated the Nuggets 186–184, combining for the most points (370) by two teams in *any* NBA game. The Pistons' 186 mark is also the record for most points by one team; obviously Denver's 184 that night is the second all-time. Denver's dynamic duo of Kiki Vandeweghe (51 points) and Alex English (47 points) teamed up for a total of 98 points in the loss. Both teams shot a combined 56.6 percent from the field and set a record for most field goals (142) made in a game. The Pistons Isiah Thomas and John Long scored 47 and 41 points respectively, making four players with 40-plus points in the game, yet another NBA record.

Other Notable Nuggets NBA Records

- Highest points-per-game average in a season (126.5) in 1981–82.

- Most consecutive games scoring 100-plus points (136) from January 21, 1981, to December 8, 1982.

- Tied for most players (6) with 1000 points in a single season: Alex English (2000), Fat Lever (1546), Michael Adams (1137), Danny Schayes (1129), Jay Vincent (1124), Blair Rasmussen (1002).

- A game against the San Antonio Spurs on January 11, 1984, produced two records: most combined points in a second half (172) and most combined points in a quarter (99), in the fourth quarter.

- Most consecutive points (26) by an individual in an NBA game, by Carmelo Anthony on December 10, 2008, against the Minnesota Timberwolves.

- Largest margin of victory in a game (58), against New Orleans on April 27, 2009.

Basketball Facts

- The classic "rainbow" logo of the Denver Nuggets was used from 1982 to 1993. To many people, it simply looked like a game of Tetris.

- Small forward Carmelo Anthony is named after his Puerto Rican–born father, who tragically died when Carmelo was just two years old.
- Only three Denver Nuggets have made it into the NBA Hall of Fame: Alex English, Dan Issel and David Thompson.

Retired Numbers

- 2, Alex English, F, 1980–90
- 33, David Thompson, FG, 1975–82
- 40, Byron Beck, FC, 1967–77
- 44, Dan Issel, FC, 1976–85
- 432, Doug Moe, head coach, 1980–90 ("432" represents his total number of regular-season victories)

Top Ten Points Scored as a Denver Nugget

1. Alex English (21,645)
2. Dan Issel (16,589)
3. Carmelo Anthony (12,711)*
4. David Thompson (11,992)
5. Ralph Simpson (10,130)
6. Byron Beck (8603)
7. Fat Lever (8081)
8. Mahmoud Abdul-Rauf (7029)
9. Kiki Vandeweghe (6829)
10. Antonio McDyess (6555)

*Currently active

Chapter Five

College Sports

On-campus in Colorado

Colorado's collegiate landscape abounds with talented individuals and intriguing stories throughout the state's history. From the Fort Lewis Skyhawks in Durango to the Colorado State Rams in Fort Collins and from the flagship University of Colorado at Boulder to the Air Force Academy in Colorado Springs, the higher learning institutions of the Centennial State continually prove fertile in terms of producing top-level collegiate athletes and competition.

Ralphie's Realm

Game day at Folsom Field in Boulder offers beautiful Rocky Mountain vistas, high-quality collegiate football competition and one of the greatest pre-game traditions in the nation. Prior to each game, "Ralphie," a 1300-pound bison, leads the football team onto Folsom Field to take on their opponent. As the entire stadium rises to its feet in applause,

Ralphie and its team of handlers storm from a pen at the north end zone and complete a full lap around Folsom Field (they are known to run the 40-yard dash in five seconds flat) before being corralled again; the process is repeated at the beginning of the second half as well. This pregame stampede is notorious for striking fear in more than a few visiting players, forcing them to evade the oncoming, half-ton beast and its entourage.

Ralphie's Roots

Many fans praise the Ralphie tradition, but few know its true origins. According to the University of Colorado Athletic Department, 1934 ushered in the buffalo's first appearance after the school's newspaper, *Silver and Gold*, initiated a contest to select a new school nickname. The winning entry chose "Buffaloes" as the school's new moniker, and for the final game of the 1934 season, a group of students paid $25 to rent a buffalo calf along with a real cowboy as its keeper. The rented calf was the offspring of a famed bison named "Killer" from Trails End Ranch in Fort Collins. With the buffalo under close watch of its owner and four students on the sidelines, CU earned a 7–0 win at the University of Denver on Thanksgiving Day.

An official nationwide contest held later in 1934 cemented the University of Colorado's new nickname for good. There are mixed reports of the actual winner, but after thousands of entries were submitted from all over the country, Andrew Dickson of Boulder was named the official winner for his entry.

Prior to 1934, University of Colorado teams never possessed a singular team name but were referred to by any of the following: Silver and Gold, Silver Helmets, Yellow Jackets, Hornets, Arapahoes, Big Horns, Grizzlies and Frontiersmen.

The current tradition of Ralphie leading the team into battle began in 1966 when Ralphie I was donated to the school by John Lowery, father of a CU freshman from Lubbock, Texas. The school charged five sophomore class officers with handling the animal as it ran around the field for the "Buffalo Stomp," which literally shook the stadium. Colorado officials abruptly ended the practice, citing physical damage caused by the "stomp." Head football coach Eddie Crowder reinstituted the tradition on October 26, 1967, after the idea was brought to him, and the tradition continues today with the current installment, Ralphie V.

Both the present-day Ralphie and her predecessor, Ralphie IV, were giving to the university by billionaire media-mogul Ted Turner. The donation was a response to an article in *Bison World,* which mentioned Colorado's intention to replace Ralphie III. Thus, in 1998, Turner donated Ralphie IV from his Flying D Ranch in Montana to replace the newly retired Ralphie III. Today's Ralphie was introduced in 2007 to takeover the major mascot duties that Ralphie IV could no longer handle because of health concerns. The newer, more aggressive Ralphie was donated to Colorado from Turner's Vermejo Park Ranch in New Mexico. The two buffalo currently split duties, with Ralphie IV executing the more low-key engagements, while Ralphie V does all the running.

Byron "Whizzer" White

Despite the early success of Colorado football at the turn of the 20th century, no individual athlete took the campus and national football landscape by storm quite like Byron White. Born in Fort Collins in 1917 and raised in Wellington, White was given an academic scholarship to attend the University of Colorado. From the moment White stepped on campus he was a standout, on and off the playing field. He was used in all facets of the game. On offense, White starred at halfback but also excelled in the passing game and served as the Buff's kicker, and on defense, White was known for his aggressive and tenacious style of play. In the classroom, White was just as talented. In his senior year at Colorado, he served as student body president and was awarded a Rhodes Scholarship to attend Oxford University in England, one of the highest academic achievements bestowed upon a student.

White's greatest year on the field came in 1937 when he led the Buffaloes and college football in rushing with 1121 yards and scoring with 122 points. In fact, White's statistical totals in 1937 set national records not broken until college football teams began

COLLEGE SPORTS   115

adopting 10- and 11-game schedules years later. Colorado owned a perfect 8–0 record that season, garnering a bid to compete against Rice Universit-yin the second edition of the Cotton Bowl at season's end.

Colorado lost the bowl game 28–14, but not for a lack of effort by the "Whizzer." White connected with teammate Joe Antonio for a nine-yard touchdown pass and returned an interception 47 yards, also for a touchdown in the first quarter. White converted both extra-point kicks after the two touchdowns, thus accounting for all 14 points tallied by Colorado during the match-up.

Following the 1937 campaign, award season brought White numerous accolades, most notably becoming the University of Colorado's first All-American football player. In the Heisman voting that season, White finished second to Clint Frank of Yale, despite having a superior year statistically.

Leaving Colorado, Going Professional

After graduating from CU in 1938, Byron White was drafted and played his rookie year for the Pittsburgh Pirates (now the Steelers) of the NFL and led the league in rushing with 567 yards in 11 games. His success at Colorado and in Pittsburgh made him the highest paid player in professional football, making $15,000 per season.

White's humble nature did not couple well with the scrutiny and rigors of owning the league's richest contract. So in 1939, White left football to honor the Rhodes Scholarship previously awarded to him. He studied for one year at Oxford then returned to the NFL to play for the Detroit Lions in 1940 and 1941. White led the Lions in all offensive categories in both years, and in total he led the NFL in rushing in 1938 and 1940. In his three years as a professional, White was twice voted as a First-Team All-Pro.

White's NFL success came as no surprise to anyone who followed his collegiate career at Colorado. He was well respected as a professional player, earning praise from some of the game's great figures. In fact, long-time owner of the Pittsburgh Steelers Art Rooney said of White, "Of all the athletes I have known in my lifetime, I'd have to say Whizzer White came as close to anyone to giving 100 percent of himself when he was in competition."

Great skill, ambition and an "everyman" disposition characterized White's legacy as a collegiate and professional player and was noted by White's Pittsburgh teammate and player-coach Johnny Blood: "We had a lot rougher life in those days, but he fit right in. He was a man with a hoe, you know. He's no ivory tower person; he's no dreamer." White was distinguished by being elected to the College Football Hall of Fame in 1954.

Post-football Prominence

Byron White's football career was cut short after 1941 when he enlisted with the United States Navy

COLLEGE SPORTS

to serve in World War II. Originally, he wanted to join the ranks of the Marines but was denied because he was colorblind. White served as an intelligence officer in the Pacific Theatre of the War and even wrote the investigative report of John F. Kennedy's famous PT-109 boat incident.

After World War II, White enrolled at Yale Law School where he graduated top of his class in 1946, earning magna cum laude honors. Later, White clerked for Chief Justice Fred Vinson then practiced law in Denver for 15 years. In 1960, White lent his football celebrity to presidential candidate John F. Kennedy in an effort to win the Electoral College votes from Colorado. Although Kennedy lost in Colorado, he awarded White with the role of United States Deputy Attorney General from 1961 to 1962. White was nominated to the Supreme Court in 1962, where he served from 1962 until he retired in 1993.

As a direct result of the Whizzer's great commitment to public service, the NFL annually awards the Byron Whizzer White Award to the player who displays the greatest dedication to charity work. White was elected to the University of Colorado Athletic Hall of Fame in 1994 and was awarded the Presidential Medal of Honor by President George W. Bush in 2001. Byron White also serves as the namesake for the Tenth Circuit Federal Courthouse in Denver.

Big Eight Triumvirate

Colorado's track record as a formidable team in college football has ebbed and flowed throughout the club's history. Following the famous 1937 season, Colorado enjoyed relative success over the next 30 years, finishing atop its conference five times (1939, 1942–44, 1961), but the big, program-defining season remained elusive. That is, until 1971, when the Colorado Buffaloes ushered in numerous football firsts. The Buffs entered the season unranked, but early non-conference road victories over number nine Louisiana State University (LSU) and number six Ohio State, along with a quick 3–0 start, suddenly put Colorado football on the map. Despite the success, the toughest portion of the schedule loomed large with games against Oklahoma and Nebraska (among others) remaining. Unfortunately for CU, both games resulted in lopsided losses, but they still managed an impressive 5–2 record in Conference.

A win in the regular-season finale against in-state foe Air Force gave Colorado nine wins and an invitation from the Bluebonnet Bowl. In that game, the seventh-ranked Buffs dealt Houston (ranked 15th) a 17–10 defeat on the way to the program's first 10-win season in history. At the end of the 1971–72 season, Colorado finished third in the polls behind first-ranked Nebraska and second-place Oklahoma, the only two teams to hand the Buffs losses that season. Ultimately, 1971 was the first time that a single conference delivered the first-, second- and third-ranked teams in the final standings and, in the process, reestablished CU as a major player in college football. Colorado entered the 1972 season ranked at second, its highest preseason ranking ever.

Reaching the Summit

The 1989–90 season saw the Buffaloes come within a single victory of winning college football's ultimate prize, the National Championship. Colorado swaggered into its Orange Bowl match-up against Notre Dame with its first-ever number one ranking nationally, boasting an 11–0 record, which included impressive victories over Illinois, Washington and their archrival, Nebraska. Colorado easily captured the Big Eight title and needed to maneuver through one final obstacle on its way to claiming a perfect 12–0 record and the number one ranking in the final poll.

Unfortunately for Colorado, it could not capitalize on several scoring opportunities in the first half, and instead of placing a firm grip on Notre Dame at halftime, the teams were mired in a scoreless tie entering the second half. Notre Dame reached the end zone three times in the second half and ran away with a 21–6 Orange Bowl victory, handing Colorado its first loss of the season and a fourth-place ranking at season's end.

After squandering the school's greatest opportunity at a national title a season prior, the 1990–91 Buffaloes sought to accomplish what their predecessors could not. The team took its cues throughout the season from consensus All-American Eric "Scooter" Bieniemy, who led the nation in rushing with 1628 yards to accompany 17 touchdowns. Bieniemy went on to finish third in the Heisman vote behind Brigham Young University's Ty Detmer and Notre Dame's Raghib Ismail.

On defense, 1990 Butkus Award winner Alfred Williams was the driving force behind a defense that allowed 17.6 points per game. Colorado amassed a 10–1–1 record via wins over ranked opponents Texas (22nd), Washington (12th), Oklahoma (22nd) and Nebraska (third) and tying Tennessee (eighth). Again, Colorado won the Big Eight title and never found itself outside the top 25 the entire season, including a number one ranking the final four weeks of the season.

It was deja vu as Colorado faced familiar foe Notre Dame in the Orange Bowl in a repeat of the earlier season. Colorado would not be denied this time around. After drawing first blood with a field goal in the second quarter, the Buffaloes were forced to overcome a 9–3 deficit and lost the services of starting quarterback Darian Hagan and linebacker Kanavis McGhee in the second half. Colorado's offensive leader Eric Bieniemy scored from one yard out with 4:26 left in the third quarter, putting the Buffs ahead 10–9 for good.

Colorado ended the season with an 11–1–1 record and the number one ranking in the Associated Press, Football Writers Association of America,

National Football Federation and USA-CNN polls. Georgia Tech earned the number one vote in the United Press International poll, thus the National Championship was split between the two schools.

The Fifth Down

Colorado's first and only national championship almost never happened—save for one of the most infamous refereeing errors in college football history. Colorado's journey to the National Championship made a stop in Columbia, Missouri on October 6, 1990, for a Big Eight Conference tilt with the Tigers. Trailing 31–27, the Buffaloes had first-and-goal from the Missouri three-yard line. What transpired in the final sequence altered the course of Colorado football forever.

On first down, quarterback Charles Johnson spiked the ball to stop the clock at 28 seconds. Then, on second down, Eric Bieniemy carried the ball to the Missouri one-yard line. After the Bieniemy run, Rich Montgomery, in charge of the down-marker on the sideline, claims that linesman Ron Demaree did not tell him to change the down. Colorado then took a timeout and when play resumed, they were still on second down. Bieniemy was given the ball again–rushing for no gain. On third down, Johnson spiked the ball again to stop the clock with just two seconds remaining in the game. On the final play, the infamous fifth down, Johnson called his own number and punched the ball in for a 33–31 CU victory.

Twenty years have elapsed since the "Fifth Down Game," and those with a stake, either on the field or in the stands, still search for answers. By all accounts the error was a confluence of mistakes made by officials on the field and on the sidelines, Missouri's statistician, television and radio announcers and even the coaches and players. Ultimately, the principles involved proved completely unaware of the error made and the resulting extra play that gave Colorado the victory. According to reports, even Charles Johnson was unaware that officials had given his team a fifth down until the team returned to Boulder later that evening. The mass confusion turned into the Buffaloes' gain as they won the Big Eight, their Orange Bowl match-up against Notre Dame and eventually the 1990 National Championship.

Big Play Buffs

In 1992, Nu Skin and CoSIDA (College Sports Information Directors of America) introduced the National Play of the Year Award to the team that executed the most electrifying and unbelievable play each season. Notre Dame won the inaugural award that year, but Colorado took ownership the next two years. In 1993, it was a 34-yard halfback-option pass executed by a slipping Lamont Warren that fell into the hands of an interfered Charles Johnson for a touchdown. Colorado beat Oklahoma 27–10 on the heels of Warren and Johnson's unbelievable play, yet nobody affiliated with the "Silver and Gold" could know what was in store the following season.

It's been called the "Miracle at Michigan," and anybody who witnessed the play at the time or has seen a replay will say it's one of the greatest plays, in any sport, ever. Seventh-ranked Colorado trailed fourth-ranked Michigan 26–14 at the "Big House" with less than four minutes remaining in the game and hope waning precipitously. Colorado pulled within five points of Michigan with a touchdown at 2:16 in the fourth quarter. After a defensive stand, the Buffs got the ball back at their own 15-yard line with an impossible 85 yards to traverse in just 15 seconds. Colorado advanced the ball to its own 34-yard line with just six ticks left on the clock.

Head coach Bill McCartney called "Rocket Left"– a last ditch, Hail Mary play that had failed earlier at the end of the first half. Quarterback Kordell Stewart took the snap, bought himself time in the back-field and, with no time remaining, sailed the ball over 70 yards in the air to a cluster of receivers and defenders just short of the end zone. Colorado receiver Blake Anderson intelligently tipped the ball in the air just as a streaking Michael Westbrook dove and caught the deflection off his teammate's finger-tips. Colorado emerged triumphant over Michigan, 27–26, and in the process stunned a Wolverine throng of 106,427 in Ann Arbor along with millions watching in front of their television sets.

After the game, then-assistant coach Rick Neuheisel exclaimed, "You become a little kid. You become euphoric. You're, like, elevated. You're exploding. You look over there, and those guys are absolutely devastated and you're parading." The play earned Colorado the Excellence in Sports Performance Yearly (ESPY) award for the Play of the Year and is still considered one of the greatest plays of all time.

As if the Miracle at Michigan wasn't unbelievable enough on its own, the 1994 *Colorado Media Guide* revealed an eerie prophecy made by running back Rashaan Salaam. When asked at the beginning of the season what his favorite SportsCenter highlight would be at the end of the year, Salaam said, "It's fourth and 15 late in the game at Michigan Stadium. We're on our two-yard line, and with two seconds to go, Kordell pitches me the ball. I throw a 98-yard touchdown pass to Michael Westbrook and the Buffs win the game." Salaam was incorrect on a few of the play's details, but the coincidence is striking.

High-altitude Heisman

By 1994, only a trio of running backs—Marcus Allen (1981), Barry Sanders (1988) and Mike Rozier (1983)—amassed 2000 rushing yards in a college football season. That is, until Colorado's Rashaan Salaam made it a fourth with 2005 yards, to go along with 24 touchdowns. Both his yardage and touchdown marks led all Division I athletes and set Colorado football single-season records that stand

COLLEGE SPORTS 125

to this day. Salaam's season included four consecutive 200-yard rushing efforts, including a school record 362 yards of total offense on the road against 16th-ranked Texas. Behind the exploits of Salaam, Colorado recorded an 11–1 record in 1994 punctuated by a Fiesta Bowl victory over Notre Dame, their only loss at the hands of eventual National Champion Nebraska.

Salaam's record-setting performance on the field was handsomely rewarded in the off-season. The Buffaloes' running back won the Walter Camp, Doak Walker and Jim Brown awards before becoming the 60th Heisman Trophy Award winner. He finished 842 points ahead of the runner-up, Penn State's Ki-Jana Carter. Salaam's 1994 Heisman was Colorado's first, with only Byron Whizzer White (runner-up in 1937) and Eric Bieniemy (third place in 1990) ever approaching the award. Salaam was drafted in the first round of the 1995 NFL entry draft by the Chicago Bears and went on to play nine professional football seasons, never realizing the same success he enjoyed in 1994 as the nation's top collegiate player.

Colorado's Finest

For years, CU quarterback-turned-running-back Bobby Anderson was widely regarded as the best Colorado player ever. As a collegian, Anderson set 18 single-game season and career records along with earning All Big Eight (twice) and All-American honors. Overall, Anderson gained 2729 yards on the ground and more than 5000 yards in total offense in just three years. He was named Most Valuable Player of both the 1967 Bluebonnet Bowl and 1969 Liberty Bowl, the latter of which Anderson led CU past Alabama rushing for 254 yards and three touchdowns in his final collegiate contest.

In 1970, the Denver Broncos kept Anderson in Colorado, drafting him with their first pick (11th overall). He played with the Broncos until 1974 and played one more season, splitting 1975 with the Washington Redskins and New England Patriots. Anderson joined the Big Eight Hall of Fame in 1980, the CU All-Century Team in 1989 and in 2006 he joined his older brother, Dick, in the College Football Hall of Fame.

The First Tee: Folsom Field

Long before his three U.S. Open Championship victories and countless other tournament wins, Hale Irwin attended the University of Colorado, where he excelled on the football field and the fairways. Irwin's collegiate career began at quarterback, but he quickly moved to the defensive backfield as a cornerback for the Buffaloes. Irwin earned all Big Eight honors at the position in 1965 and 1966 after making nine interceptions. The Big Eight also recognized Irwin for his academic acumen, naming him to the conference's All-Academic Team twice while at Colorado. In 1989, Colorado honored Irwin by selecting

COLLEGE SPORTS

him as one of its 25-member All-Century Team, standing shoulder to shoulder with the likes of Byron White, Joe Romig, Dick Anderson and Eric Bieniemy, among others.

Undoubtedly, Irwin's fame is directly linked to his golfing prowess, something that was on display early in Boulder. Irwin won consecutive Big Eight golfing titles in 1966 and 1967, adding the overall individual NCAA Championship (also in 1967) to his extensive resumé of Colorado accomplishments. Irwin still owns Colorado's record for single-season stroke average at 71.86, which he achieved in his junior season. Irwin turned professional after graduating in 1967 and went on to an illustrious golfing career, which included three U.S. Open titles (1974, 1979 and 1990), five Ryder Cup appearances for the United States, 20 PGA Tour and 45 Championship Tour tournament victories.

Irwin was voted the 19th greatest golfer of all time by *Golf Digest* and was inducted into the World Golf Hall of Fame in 1992. He is another shining example of the diverse, world-class talent produced by the University of Colorado.

Triple Threat

Dave Logan shone as a basketball and football standout at the University of Colorado from 1972 to 1975 after receiving over 200 scholarship offers from universities nationwide. Logan chose the University of Colorado over other institutions and Major League

Baseball after being drafted by the Cincinnati Reds his senior year of high school. Later, the Cleveland Browns (NFL) and the Sacramento Kings (NBA) drafted Logan following his collegiate career at Colorado. Being drafted to three professional leagues is a feat Logan shares with two other athletes: Dave Winfield and Mickey McCarty. Currently, Logan can be heard doing play-by-play for the Denver Broncos, and he hosts a sports talk show on KOA.

Other University of Colorado Highlights

- The Colorado Buffaloes football team claims 31 Consensus All-Americans in the school's history.

- Five Buffaloes have been inducted into the College Football Hall of Fame: Byron White (1952), Joe Romig (1984), Dick Anderson (1993), Bobby Anderson (2006) and Alfred Williams (2010).

- The Colorado ski team owns an astounding 17 NCAA Championships (1959, 1960, 1972–79, 1982, 1991, 1995, 1998, 1999, 2006 and 2011).

- Jimmy Heuga, a member of CU's 1959 National Champion ski team, won the bronze medal in the slalom event at the 1964 Innsbruck Winter Olympic Games.

- Men's and women's cross-country have won five NCAA championship titles.

- Bill Toomey holds the distinction of being the only CU Athlete to win an individual gold medal

COLLEGE SPORTS 129

at the Olympics. Toomey triumphed in the decathlon at the 1968 Mexico City Summer Games, setting a record of 8193 points at the time. Toomey was a two-time All-American in the pentathlon while at CU and was voted the 1966 Amateur Athlete of the Year.

- As a member of the CU track and field team in 1936, Gil Cruter twice broke the world high jump record, surpassing 6 feet 10 inches.

- The first CU Olympian was track-and-field athlete David Bolen, a member of the 1948 U.S. Olympic team.

Pioneer Prowess

Thirty miles to the southeast, the Denver Pioneers aren't so much concerned about football as their neighbors in Boulder. That's because at Denver University, hockey trumps all else. The "Pios" find themselves in national championship discussions annually, despite DU's status as a private institution and its small enrollment (11,600 students in 2010) relative to other national powers. DU is tied with WCHA (Western Collegiate Hockey Association) rival, University of North Dakota, for second in all-time NCAA hockey championships with seven. Only the mark set by the University of Michigan (9) usurps the prodigious accomplishments of Denver and North Dakota.

Throughout history, 24 Pioneers went on to play professionally in the NHL. Most notably, Glenn

Anderson (Edmonton Oilers), Keith Magnuson (Chicago Blackhawks), Kevin Dineen (Hartford/Philadelphia/Carolina) and Craig Patrick (Washington/California) all played their collegiate hockey at DU. Patrick was also the architect of the 1991 and 1992 Stanley Cup champion Pittsburgh Penguins as the team's general manager. Other Pioneer alumni currently playing in the NHL include Colorado Avalanche forward Paul Stastny, Maple Leafs Tyler Bozak and 2006 Hobey Baker Award winner, Matt Carle of the Philadelphia Flyers.

The Chief

In December 2010, Denver Pioneer hockey and the game at-large lost one of its most iconic and successful coaches in history. Murray Armstrong, better known to many as "The Chief," passed away at the age of 94 after a string of strokes severely affected his health. Armstrong's 40-year-long hockey career was as distinguished as any other person fortunate enough to play and coach the game.

Armstrong joined the Pioneers in 1956 after a nine-year NHL career (playing with the Maple Leafs and Red Wings, among others) and another nine seasons coaching the Regina Pats in Canada's junior hockey system. As an interesting historical footnote, late in Armstrong's playing days with the Detroit Red Wings, general manager Jack Adams relegated the veteran forward in favor of an up-and-coming 18-year-old named Gordie Howe. Upon

COLLEGE SPORTS

arriving in Denver, Armstrong assured the Pioneer community of an NCAA Championship within just three years. Armstrong proved to be wrong—it took him only two years to deliver on the promise as DU defeated North Dakota 6–2 on the way to earning its first hockey title.

As the hockey program progressed, Armstrong delivered again and again. His teams took college hockey's highest prize with championships in 1958, 1960, 1961, 1968 and 1969. Armstrong's final championship is particularly exceptional as it came against future NHL Hall of Fame goaltender Ken Dryden who backstopped the Cornell Big Red throughout his collegiate days. The championship pitted the previous two title winners against each other (Cornell, 1967; DU, 1968) in a struggle to establish dominance over college hockey. Dryden received top billing entering the game, but Denver's Gerry Powers was equal to the task as both goalies frustrated the opposition's offense throughout the game. Ultimately, two Denver goals in the third period proved the difference as the Pioneers captured their fifth title and Armstrong's last.

A former *Denver Post* reporter who formally covered The Chief during his coaching days remarked of his career, "He has been to college hockey what only a handful ever are to other sports—a John Wooden to basketball, for instance, a Woody Hayes or Bear Bryant to football. An era ends. We won't see another like him." In total, Armstrong led Denver to

11 Frozen Four Tournament appearances (five times a champion and three times runner-up), eight WCHA Conference titles along with 463 career wins over his remarkable 21 years as DU's head coach. He was twice voted WCHA Coach of the Year.

Armstrong inherited a fledgling Denver hockey program that joined the Division I level in 1949—they had won a paltry 12 games the season before he joined DU's ranks. In Armstrong's first year at the helm, Denver equaled its win total of the previous season, but beginning in year two, the team began cementing itself as an elite program in the world of college hockey. The Pioneers served notice to the rest of college hockey when they won in 1958 and went on a tear throughout the next two decades. They defeated all takers-on, both in the college ranks and several national teams while contesting international tournament warm-ups. Throughout his 21-year coaching career that spanned three decades, Armstrong-led teams posted a .674 winning percentage and an overall record of 463–215–31. He was voted the National Coach of the Year in 1961.

Since Armstrong's departure in 1977, four men have served as head coach of Denver Hockey, but none quite so successfully as The Chief. In the words of current DU coach, George Gwozdecky, "The game of hockey and the University of Denver has lost one of its great men. Coach Armstrong was the legendary architect of this great DU Pioneer hockey program."

A Fine Year

In terms of a singular college hockey team, very few rival the 1960–61 Denver Pioneers. During that season, DU posted an otherworldly record of 30–1 on its way to the school's second NCAA Championship. But it was the other on-ice accomplishments in 1960 that truly set the team apart. In February of that season, Denver faced the United States National Team in an Olympic warm-up leading into the Squaw Valley Games. In a two-game miniseries, DU earned a 7–5 victory in the first game and skated to a 5–5 tie in the second game against the eventual gold medalists at the 1960 Winter Olympics.

Just two days later, the Soviet Union came calling, and on that night, Denver was up to the task, tying the powerhouse 2–2 (DU also tied the USSR 4–4 in 1959) at a time when the Soviets began an unprecedented reign of dominance over international ice hockey. From 1954 to 1991, the Soviet Union won 19 World Championships and seven Olympic gold medals. Throughout that same Olympic warm-up season, Denver also defeated both the West German and Swedish national teams in relatively easy fashion. Later in life, the legendary Denver coach joked, "We tied the U.S. team and beat them, and didn't lose a game down there, so I figured we had a pretty good team that year."

In March 1961, Denver capped off its phenomenal season by capturing the WCHA tournament title with a win over rival Colorado College 3–1 and eventually being crowned National Champion with a victory against Michigan Tech. In the years to come, the Pioneers would win five more National Championships and face several more national teams, but the 1960 campaign remained unprecedented and unparalleled by all other Denver teams.

Bill Masterton

Several Pioneers created enduring legacies over their collegiate and professional careers, but none quite like Bill Masterton, albeit in a somber and grave manner. Masterton earned three letters at DU and two All-American honors, and he served as the Pios captain during the 1960–61 season and was a critical component of DU's back-to-back National Championship teams those same two years. Masterton posted 80 points in 32 games in 1961, an NCAA record at the time, and was voted Most Outstanding Player of the 1961 Frozen Four. He still ranks third (tied with John McMillan) in points with 196 (66 goals, 130 assists) and second in assists all-time in Pioneer history.

Masterton's college achievements prompted the Montreal Canadiens to sign him after the 1961 season, but he never became a fixture with the Habs or in the NHL overall. He languished in the minor leagues until retiring in 1963, after which time he obtained a Masters's degree from Denver University and then worked in corporate America for the Honeywell Corporation in Minneapolis, all the while

COLLEGE SPORTS   135

still playing as an amateur for the U.S. National Team.

When the NHL expanded to the Twin Cities in 1967, the Minnesota North Stars promptly signed Bill Masterton, offering him another chance at a professional hockey career. The season started with great frenzy for Masterton as he scored the franchise's first goal in the team's history, against the St. Louis Blues on October 11, 1967.

The North Star forward's most lasting legacy wasn't made until January 13, 1968, as Minnesota took on the Oakland Seals at the Met Center in Bloomington, Minnesota. With four minutes expired in the first period, Masterton streaked into the Oakland end and delivered a pass to line-mate Wayne Connolly. As everyone in the arena followed the pass and ensuing action, Masterton lost his balance and fell backward onto the ice, the full force of the descent absorbed by his head. The impact with the ice was so fierce that Masterton immediately began bleeding from his nose and ears, a gruesome scene indeed. As trainers and teammates rushed to his aid, one player recounted Masterton's words as he lay injured: "Never again, never again"—then he lost consciousness.

Thirty short hours later, Masterton died from what doctors called a "massive brain injury," becoming the first NHL player to die as a direct result of an on-ice incident. Lou Nanne, Masterton's teammate with the North Stars, said of his friend's death, "People in the NHL didn't get to see what Bill could do, but he was a special player." Following Masterton's death, more NHL players began voluntarily wearing helmets (not required at the time), and the argument for compulsory head protection in the NHL became more feverish, with the league finally enacting a mandatory helmet edict in 1979.

The NHL began awarding the Bill Masterton Memorial Trophy in 1968 to the player who best exhibits, "to a high degree the qualities of perseverance, sportsmanship, and dedication to hockey." Former winners include some of the "who's who" of the NHL, such as Bobby Clarke (1972), Rod Gilbert (1976), Pat LaFontaine (1995), Mario Lemieux (1993), Teemu Selanne (2006) and Steve Yzerman (2003). Denver University also gives out the Bill Masterton Award to the Pioneers' Most Valuable Player each season.

Elite Company

Current Pioneer head coach George Gwozdecky holds a unique distinction that separates him from the fraternity of NCAA hockey coaches, past and present. Gwozdecky is the only man in the sport's history to win an NCAA hockey title as a player, assistant coach and head coach. The Pios' bench-boss lettered four times as a winger for the University of Wisconsin along with winning the 1977 NCAA Championship in his college-playing days. His coach at Wisconsin was the legendary "Badger" Bob Johnson, who also coached Colorado College from 1963 to 1966.

COLLEGE SPORTS

After college, Gwozdecky won another NCAA crown, this time serving as an assistant coach for the 1986 Michigan State Spartans before becoming the Pioneers' head coach in 1994. At Michigan State, "Gwoz," as he is known, had the opportunity to refine his craft under the tutelage of college hockey's all-time winning coach, Ron Mason (924).

During Gwoz's tenure, Pioneer teams have earned thirteen separate 20-win seasons, including the 2004 and 2005 NCAA Championships. Gwozdecky's earlier career was distinguished by an NAIA (National Association of Intercollegiate Athletics) title, won in 1983 as coach of the University of Wisconsin-River Falls. In terms of individual honors, Gwozdecky is well decorated, twice the winner of the Spencer Penrose Award as the Nation's Top Hockey Coach as voted by the American Hockey Coaches Association. The Pios coach also holds memberships in the Wisconsin Hockey Hall of Fame and the Northwestern Ontario Sports Hall of Fame, and he was inducted into the Miami University "Cradle of Coaches" Hall of Fame in 2006 for his five years of service as the Redhawks' head coach prior to his current stint in Denver.

Gwozdecky's former athletic director at Miami University explains why the head coach has achieved his high level of career success: "What makes George such a successful coach is his ability to motivate and get the most out of his players. His teams are always focused and ready to play, and that is a direct reflection of the leadership that he provides."

The Best Ever

The first decade of the new millennium was particularly successful for the Denver University ski team. With its third consecutive NCAA Championship in 2010, Denver capped off a decade of competition that resulted in a total of seven national titles. The latest skiing championship is the 21st in Denver history, situating the Pioneers as the most victorious ski team in NCAA history as well as being the fourth most successful NCAA sports team of any kind behind Oklahoma State wrestling (34), USC track and field (26) and Iowa wrestling (22). When combined with the school's seven hockey championships, Denver boasts a total of 28 NCAA titles, a record that stands eighth in NCAA history.

Denver won the first four NCAA ski championships from 1954 to 1957, when it was only competed as a men's sport, and after a three-year hiatus from the podium, the Pioneers won seven straight titles from 1961 to 1967. Another three-peat came from 1969 to 1971, but Denver would be stuck on 14 titles for 29 years until it won again in 2000, which jumpstarted the Pioneers on their latest run of championships.

Other Denver University Notes

- Denver University boasts more than 200 All-Americans and 56 Olympians in its illustrious history.
- Olympic figure skating silver and gold medalist and five-time World Champion and U.S. Olympic

figure skating star Michelle Kwan graduated from DU in 2009.

- Comedian and actor Sinbad played basketball at DU under his real name of David Adkins.

- From the 1860s to the early 1920s, Denver went without a nickname but took on the names "Ministers" or "Fighting Parsons" given by local writers in respect to the school's Methodist heritage. Denver did not become the "Pioneers" until 1925, as the result of a student nickname contest.

- DU's first football game was against Colorado College in 1885. According to the Colorado College Athletic Department, the game is believed to be the first intercollegiate football game played west of the Mississippi River.

- Denver University's first athletic event was a baseball game in 1867 against the Arapahoe Baseball Club.

A Small School with Big Success

The "Battle for the Gold Pan" is the name given to the classic, annual rivalry game held between the Colorado College Tigers and the Denver Pioneers. The in-state foes, separated by just 65 miles, have played each other every year since 1949, but the tradition of bestowing the Gold Pan Trophy to the winner of the game started in 1993. Colorado College leads the overall series 10–7 at the conclusion of the 2009–10 season.

Success has always been the calling card of Colorado College, whose ice hockey program commenced through sponsorship via benevolent local business firms in Colorado Springs. The school's inaugural game in 1938 resulted in a lopsided 8–1 loss to "Giddings Department Store," one of the other seven teams created along with Colorado College constituting the Pikes Peak Hockey League. Notwithstanding a lackluster first season, Colorado College rapidly gained success on the national stage, and by 1948 it began hosting the NCAA Championship Tournament at the Broadmoor Ice Palace—the school's home arena. The tournament was originally a partnership between Colorado College and the Broadmoor Hotel, which converted its underutilized equestrian center into an ice arena for the Tigers when the program started.

Colorado College emerged victorious at the third edition of the tournament in 1950 and again in 1957 (defeating perennial powers Boston University and Michigan, respectively), giving the Tigers an astonishing two national championships in just nine years. Yet, the past 63 years have proved unkind to Colorado College, as no Tiger team has reached the pinnacle of college hockey again. Although another title has remained elusive, Colorado College boasts a resumé rife with other successes. The school boasts 19 NCAA tournament berths, 10 Frozen Four appearances (five times competing in the final game, posting a 2–3 record) and nine regular season conference titles.

Colorado College Notes

- A total of 60 Colorado College hockey players have been named All-Americans throughout the program's history.

- Twenty Tigers have represented their country at the World Championships and/or the Olympics. Additionally, 30 former Colorado College players have made it to the NHL ranks, including Jack Hillen, Curtis McElhinney and Marc Stuart.

- NHL Hall of Fame head coach "Badger" Bob Johnson coached Colorado College hockey from 1963 to 1966. Currently, the school hands out the Bob Johnson Award annually to the team's most outstanding freshman.

Commanding the Competition

Each year, the United States' Service Academies (the Army Black Knights, the Navy Midshipmen and the Air Force Falcons) compete for what is called the "Commander-in-Chief's Trophy." The award is given to the school with the best record after the three football teams face each other head-to-head throughout the college football season.

The competition was the brainchild of Air Force General George Simler and was first introduced in 1972 when President Richard Nixon occupied the White House. The award is named after one of the president's roles as Commander-in-Chief of the United States' Armed Forces. Simler, who died the same year the competition began, served as Air Force's athletic director during his distinguished career.

The 2010 college football season marked the 39th edition of the Commander-in-Chief's competition, and the Air Force Academy, located in Colorado Springs, won for the 17th time. Air Force took the trophy away from Navy, which held it since 2003. Previously, Air Force owned bragging rights from 1997 to 2002 and, prior to that, from 1989 to 1995. Overall, the Falcons hold the all-time edge against its fellow service members Navy (12) and Army (6). The title has been shared four times since its inception.

Air Force Facts

- The Falcons came within one win against Brigham Young University from playing for the National Championship in 1985. Air Force peaked at number two that season under the guidance of coach Fisher DeBerry and finished number five after a 12–1 overall record and a win over Texas in the Bluebonnet Bowl.

- Air Force and Colorado State University, its neighbor to the north in Fort Collins, annually battle for the Ram-Falcon Trophy, in which the Falcons own a 17–13 overall lead in the 30 years since the tradition began in 1980.

- Legendary NFL coach Bill Parcells got his first head coaching gig with Air Force in 1978, after

COLLEGE SPORTS

years of serving as an assistant for several other programs. He lasted only one year at the Academy, posting a 3–8 record.

- Falcon Chance Harridge set the NCAA Division I record for rushing touchdowns in a season by a quarterback (23) in 2002. The record was tied in 2003 by current Broncos quarterback and former Florida star Tim Tebow and then broken by Navy's Ricky Dobbs in 2009 (27).

- Another former Falcon, Beau Morgan, was the first player in NCAA Division I history to rush and pass for 1000 yards in two different seasons (1995 and 1996). Morgan also holds the Division I record for the most yards rushed by a quarterback in a single season, with 1494 yards gained on 225 attempts. In regard to his dual-threat disposition, Morgan said, "The challenge is to have the aggressive mindset that you want to run the ball and, at the same time, on the next play, having the composure and discernment to sit in the pocket and deliver a strike."

- Although Jack Dempsey owns the vast majority of pugilistic headlines in the state of Colorado, the Air Force Falcons boxing team deserves a great deal of credit. The team owns 18 National Collegiate Boxing Championships—that's 13 more than the next team, Navy, which is a five-time champion.

The Bronze Boot

Every year, Colorado State football finds itself in a trio of rivalry games, two of which come against the in-state adversaries of Colorado (Rocky Mountain Showdown) and Air Force (Ram-Falcon Trophy). However, these two battles pale in comparison to the standoff that takes place against the Wyoming Cowboys located in Laramie. Considered one of the oldest football rivalries west of the Mississippi River, the two schools, separated by just 60 miles over the Colorado-Wyoming border, have battled each other since 1899. It's certainly the oldest rivalry for both the Cowboys and Rams (known as the Aggies back then) and it spans three centuries.

Originally, the game was dubbed "The Border War," and many still refer to it as such, but in 1968 the ROTC groups on both campuses began the Bronze Boot tradition. Starting that year, and every year since, the visiting school's ROTC relays the game ball to the shared border where the host counterpart receives the ball and runs it the remainder of the distance and eventually into the stadium. Since the Bronze Boot's inception, Colorado State is 21–22 against rival Wyoming, but overall it leads the series 54–42–5 (there were 12 years in which the game was not contested).

Six Times Gold

In 2008, Englewood's Amy Van Dyken was inducted into the United States Olympic Committee (USOC) Hall of Fame, the culmination of a spectacular swimming career on the world's biggest stage. At an early age, Van Dyken suffered from severe asthma and was introduced to competitive swimming when doctors recommended she strengthen her lungs by taking up the sport. Despite the disease, and in many ways because of it, Van Dyken is currently regarded as one of the all-time greatest female American Olympians.

She was a state champion at Cherry Creek High School, but her career jump-started when she transferred to Colorado State University after two years at the University of Arizona. She broke the United States' record in the 50-yard freestyle event with a time of 21.77 seconds to take gold at the 1994 NCAA National Swimming Championships. At the end of the season she received her first of many honors, being named the NCAA Female Swimmer of the Year.

Van Dyken rode the momentum of her phenomenal collegiate season and began training full time at the United States Olympic Committee (USOC) Training Center in Colorado Springs to prepare for the 1996 Atlanta Olympics. Leaving college early proved to be the best move of Van Dyken's career as, in Atlanta, she became the first American woman to win four gold medals at a single edition of the Olympics: the 50-meter freestyle, 4x100 freestyle relay, 100-meter butterfly and the 4x100-meter medley relay. Van Dyken triumphed while battling cramps and other ailments throughout the games—something she became accustomed to as a young swimmer overcoming asthma.

Following her success in Atlanta, Van Dyken was named the USOC and Associated Press Female Athlete of the Year and the Female Swimmer of the Year by USA Swimming. She also won the ESPY for top Female Athlete of the Year, along with several other distinctions. In addition, Van Dyken took on celebrity status by making several appearances on TV talk shows, magazine covers and commercial advertisements. Despite her newfound fame and success, Van Dyken returned to Colorado State University to finish her collegiate studies.

While the world was seemingly at Van Dyken's fingertips post-Atlanta, a weight-lifting mishap in 1998 severely injured her shoulder (tearing the labrum) and threatened to keep her out of the pool permanently. But the swimmer, famous for her dogged determination, turned the setback into opportunity and mounted a comeback at the 2000 Sydney Olympics that defied the odds. Although she was unable to train for a full year while her shoulder healed, Van Dyken qualified for three events at the Sydney Games. She captured gold twice in Australia, again in the 4x100 freestyle relay and the 4x100-meter medley relay events, which brought her career Olympic medal haul to six gold medals (also accompanied by six World Championship gold medals won throughout her career).

Currently, Van Dyken's six gold medals rank her sixth among all female American Olympians in history and eighth among all American Olympians historically, male or female. Jenny Thompson is the only female American swimmer to win more Olympic gold medals (8) than Van Dyken.

Domineering Demeanor

Although 2000 brought continued success for Amy Van Dyken, it also put the swimmer through a public relations nightmare. At the Sydney Games, Van Dyken spit into the swimming lane of Inge de Bruijn, following a loss to her rival. To compound the problem, Van Dyken infamously quipped, "I could win the race too, if I were a man." Van Dyken drew the ire of many fans and supporters and was even ranked in *Sports Illustrated*'s list of most unsportsmanlike conduct at the Olympics. Her actions, although out of line, were a product of her notoriously strong competitive spirit.

Van Dyken's well-known intimidation tactics of grunting at, staring down and spitting in the direction of competitors often drew criticism throughout her career and overshadowed her incredible talent and skill. John Mattos, her coach at Colorado State, said of her fierce mentality, "If you could bust inside Amy's head in the moments before the race, it might be frightening what you would find." But Van Dyken had her own response to the pundits: "Competitors aren't my friends. You're not swimming for yourself or your swim club anymore. You're competing for the entire country. If I don't do my best at the Olympics, I have to wait four years. That's a lot of pressure."

Today, Van Dyken's involvement in the community and her motivational speaking activities have erased the memory of her unsavory antics as a swimmer. She is married to former University of Colorado and Denver Broncos punter Tom Rouen, and the two reside in both Colorado and Arizona. Van Dyken has since been inducted into the Colorado Sports Hall of Fame and the International Swimming Hall of Fame to go along with her USOC Hall of Fame induction. For all of her accomplishments, *Sports Illustrated* named her the 39th greatest female athlete in United States' history.

Chapter Six

Winter Sports and the Olympics

Breckenridge Beginnings

The discovery of gold in 1858 and the ensuing "Pike's Peak Gold Rush" attracted hordes of miners to the Rocky Mountains who initially set up camp along rivers where deposits were most accessible. Traversing Colorado's terrain presented difficulties to settlers whose webbed snowshoes were ill equipped to manage the volume and depth of the area's powdered snow.

According to the Colorado Ski and Snowboard Museum, the first documented ski usage occurred in 1859 along the Blue River near Breckenridge when miners sought to navigate the treacherous topography of the region. Approximately 10 men skied from their location on the Blue River to a new area they would christen "Eldora West." The museum also asserts that by the winter of 1860, "...all provisions were being carried over the range from South Park to Georgia Gulch by men on skis." Little did these miners know the lasting impact their maiden skiing would have today on the millions who frequent Colorado's slopes annually.

Postal Progress

Skiing remained a functional endeavor for several years following its 1860 inception, mainly as the preferred mode of transportation of U.S. Postal Service carriers. Men like Father Dyer, a fervent pastor turned mail carrier, skied vast distances to ensure that mail service extended to even the most remote Colorado locations. Dyer's scribing, *The Snowshoe Itinerant*, provided an insider's view of this arduous task and his near-fatal avalanche encounter. It is reported that by 1880, roughly 50 carriers serviced Colorado, braving the harshest of conditions in carrying out their critical task. Some credit Colorado's rapid expansion to the postal service, which permitted correspondence when snow stymied other traditional methods of transportation.

The Joy of Skiing

More leisurely and recreational skiing emerged in the late 19th century, as Coloradoans organized ski parties, cross-country races and winter carnivals. According to the Colorado Ski and Snowboard Museum, young and old alike took part in the revelry of skiing, tobogganing and skating in the mountain towns of Telluride and Steamboat Springs. By this time, skiing had entrenched itself as not only a useful method of transportation but also as a means of enjoyment.

In 1911, competitive skiing began in Colorado when Norwegian immigrant Carl Howelsen demonstrated ski jumping to Coloradoans, a sport he championed in his native Norway. Upon witnessing his aerodynamic artistry, Steamboat Springs residents began calling Howelsen "The Flying Norseman," paying homage to his Scandinavian roots. His inculcation of skiing and ski jumping in Colorado earned him a permanent name at Steamboat Springs ski jumping hill, named "Howelsen Hill" in his honor. Howelsen is also a member of the Colorado Ski and Snowboard Hall of Fame for his many contributions to the state's skiing history.

Tenth Mountain Division

Colorado welcomed the United States Military during World War II for special winter and mountain training, commencing a lasting legacy of destination skiing in one of the world's pre-eminent resort towns. In the Finnish Winter War of 1939, the undermanned Finns (by some accounts five to one) held off the Russians for three months by using quick strikes on skis, guerilla warfare tactics and special winter survival methods. Recognizing the Finns' success, and with war looming, the United States Army sent the Tenth Light Division to Camp Hale to begin preparing for the possibility of winter and mountain combat.

Located just 30 miles from Vail, Camp Hale provided the perfect environment for troops to hone their high-altitude and sub-zero skiing, along with climbing and survival skills. The Tenth was commissioned to fight in Europe and suffered casualties but quickly became one of the most decorated military divisions. Besides bringing a strong sense of state pride for their contribution to the war, members of the Tenth Mountain Division further benefited Colorado by creating the Vail Ski Resort in 1962.

Tenth Division members Pete Seibert and Earl Eaton created the resort in a location they remembered skiing while training for the war. During military training, the two men had skied many of the areas around Camp Hale, such as Keystone, Loveland and Aspen, and it was then that they discovered a ski spot outfitted with the perfect peak-and-basin combination. Originally calling it "No Name Mountain," Seibert and Eaton opened Vail Ski Resort just six months after commencing construction. The resort's overwhelming popularity led to rapid growth and success, and today it is the second largest ski resort behind Whistler-Blackcomb in British Columbia.

Little Big Town

Obtaining the designation "Ski Town U.S.A." is no small accomplishment, especially for a place like Steamboat Springs, a town of just 12,000 residents. Steamboat Springs' moniker is well deserved, sending a record-setting 79 Winter Olympians to 17 Olympic Games starting with Ski Jumper John Steele in 1932. The athletes were either originally from Steamboat or spent time on its slopes training for the Olympics; in all, Olympians with Steamboat ties have represented 11 different countries in almost every discipline imaginable. There is no other municipality in North America able to boast such robust Olympic attendance. With one out of every 145 Steamboat Springs residents being an Olympian, the city exclaims, "…you're just as likely to share the gondola with an Olympian, as you are to be in the checkout line with one."

Two critical components provide the foundation for Steamboat's unrivaled winter sport success: the city's Winter Sports Club and the aforementioned Howelsen Hill. In fact, all but one American to medal in either Olympic Ski Jumping or Nordic Combined spent time training at Howelsen in Steamboat Springs. The mountain town is also considered the birthplace of freestyle skiing in America, as the new style gained footing in the 1970s.

Coloradoans at the Olympics

Colorado's mountainous topography and snow-filled winters provide fertile training ground for amateur winter athletes seeking to reach the pinnacle of their sport—Olympic gold. The sheer volume of Colorado athletes boasting an Olympic resumé is astonishing, but a few individuals stand above the rest:

• **Edward Patrick Francis "Eddie" Eagan (Denver):** Eddie Eagan is one of only four people with a medal from both the Summer and Winter Olympic Games. Eagan captured the light-heavyweight boxing gold medal at the 1920 Antwerp Summer Games and subsequently won another gold medal in the four-man bobsleigh event at the 1932 Lake Placid Games. Eagan holds the unique distinction of being the *only* person in history to win gold medals at both the Summer and Winter editions of the Olympics. A student at Yale Law and a Rhodes Scholar at Oxford, Eagan joined the U.S. Bar Association in 1932 and was a colonel in the U.S. Army during World War II. He died in 1967 in Rye, New York, and 16 years later was posthumously elected to the inaugural class of the U.S. Olympic Hall of Fame.

• **Lindsey Kildow-Vonn (Vail):** Lindsey Kildow-Vonn, better known by her married name "Vonn," was born in Minnesota but grew up training in Vail before permanently moving to the Colorado Mountains in the late 1990s. Vonn's accomplishments are simply staggering. She has won two Olympic Alpine medals and has more than 40 World Cup Circuit victories, making her the most successful female American Alpine skier in history. Vonn is married to former U.S. Ski teammate Thomas Vonn, and the couple lives in Vail in the off-season.

• **Anders Haugen (Dillon):** A native of Norway, Haugen was an accomplished ski jumper and captained the 1924 U.S. Olympic Ski Team at the Olympics in Chamonix, France. Haugen finished fourth, but an error found 50 years later revealed that the third-place finisher's score was incorrectly recorded. Thus, Haugen switched positions with Thorleif Haug (Norway), receiving a bronze medal five decades later! Haug's daughter respectfully delivered the

WINTER SPORTS AND THE OLYMPICS   155

medal to its rightful owner. Haugen, who immigrated to the U.S. in 1908, is the only American to win an Olympic ski jumping medal and is a member of the Colorado Ski and Snowboard Hall of Fame as of 1978.

• **Chris Klug (Vail):** Part of the U.S. Snowboard Team in 1998, 2002 and 2010, Klug won bronze at the Salt Lake City Games in the men's parallel giant slalom event. The medal is not the real story, however, as Klug received a liver transplant in 2000 to cure his primary sclerosing cholangitis. Klug made a full recovery from the surgery and became the only transplant recipient to compete in the Olympics, winning his Olympic bronze medal just two years later!

• **Toby Dawson (Vail):** Born Kim Bong-Seok and adopted by a Vail couple, Dawson won a bronze medal in freestyle skiing at the 2006 Torino Games. He was adopted after being separated from his mother at a market in Korea when he was only three, never to see his biological parents again. That is, until 2007, when someone recognized his photo from the 2006 Olympics, which led to a reunion with his biological father and brother.

• **Bill Demong/Todd Lodwick/Johnny Spillane (Steamboat Springs):** The trio took the Nordic Combined world by storm and captivated America at the 2010 Vancouver Winter Olympic Games. Demong became the first American to win gold in a Nordic event when he finished first in the 10k Large Hill race in Vancouver, finishing ahead of Steamboat teammate Johnny Spillane who captured silver in the competition. Spillane followed up silver in the Large Hill event with another silver in the Normal Hill race.

Technically, Spillane became the first American to win an Olympic medal in the sport of Nordic Combined, while Demong was the first to win gold in the sport. They joined forces with fellow Steamboater Todd Lodwick and Park City, Utah, native Brett Camerota to win the silver medal in the Nordic team event. That gave Spillane three silver medals for the Games, Demong a gold and silver and Lodwick his first-ever Olympic medal. Quite unexpectedly, an American medaled in every single Nordic Combined event at the 2010 Games, not to mention that these were the United States' first-ever Olympic medals in the sport of Nordic Combined! By competing in Vancouver, Lodwick also became Steamboat's only five-time Olympian (1994–2010).

• **Nelson Carmichael (Steamboat Springs):** With Steamboat Springs boasting the first freestyle skiing in America, it was appropriate that Carmichael became Colorado's first Olympic mogul medalist. He reached the podium at the 1992 Albertville Games, winning bronze in the freestyle event.

• **Shannon Dunn-Downing (Steamboat Springs):** Also from Steamboat Springs, Dunn-Downing, who attended the University of Colorado during her college days, was the first American woman to win an Olympic snowboarding medal—a bronze in the halfpipe event at the 1998 Nagano Winter Olympics.

• **Katie Uhlaender (Vail):** Two-time Olympic skeleton racer (2006, 2010), Uhlaender is attempting to become a dual Winter and Summer Olympics competitor. Uhlaender, from Vail and now Breckenridge, is in training to compete in weightlifting at the 2012 London Summer Games.

• **Gretchen Bleiler (Aspen):** From Aspen, Bleiler is a four-time gold medalist in the X-Games' super-pipe event and a silver medalist in the Olympic halfpipe event, which she won at the 2006 Torino Games. She began competing at 11 and is considered one of snowboarding's foremost ambassadors.

• **Paul Stastny (Denver):** Colorado Avalanche forward and former Denver University Pioneer, Stastny won a silver medal at the 2010 Vancouver Olympic Ice Hockey Tournament as a member of the United States' Ice Hockey Team. Stastny's upstart American squad shocked the world in reaching the gold medal match against North American rival Canada, just to fall short on an overtime game-winning goal by Sidney Crosby in one of the most thrilling games in Olympic ice hockey history. The Avalanche star finished the 2010 tournament with one goal and two assists for three points, a plus-two rating and eight shots in six games.

Other Winter Sports Notes

- Andrea Mead Lawrence, who went on to live in Aspen and serve on the town's planning board, was the first American to win double gold at a single Olympics. Lawrence captured gold in both the slalom and giant slalom at the 1952 Oslo Games.

- Colorado transplants Billy Kidd and Jimmy Heuga won the United States its first-ever Olympic Alpine medals, taking silver and bronze in the slalom at the 1964 Innsbruck Olympics.

- Cindy Nelson, whose father served in the Tenth Mountain Division near Vail, is considered one of the United States' first great downhill skiers. She won the downhill bronze at the 1976 Games.

- As reported by the Colorado Ski and Snowboard Museum, the state has 143 defunct resorts. Locations such as "Climax," "Conquistador's" and "Montezuma Basin" are all examples of once operational skiing destinations now gone by the wayside.

An Olympics Lost

The year 1976 was meant to be a major showcase for the city of Denver and the State of Colorado. The United States was in the midst of celebrating its bicentennial and the Centennial State was supposed to host the XII Winter Olympic Games.

WINTER SPORTS AND THE OLYMPICS

"Supposed to" because the International Olympic Committee (IOC) awarded Denver the rights to the 1976 Winter Games in May 1970, but a statewide vote in 1972 resulted in a 60–40 consensus against serving as Olympic host. The opposition's landslide victory made Denver, Colorado and the United States the first city, state and country to ever reject an Olympic hosting honor.

The strong dissent against the $5-million-bond measure sharply contrasted with the image two-and-a-half years earlier, where a hero's welcome met the Denver Organizing Committee returning from Amsterdam with bid in hand. The welcome was even adorned with a small motorcade and a brass band providing fanfare. That's when the opposing side, led by lawyer Dick Lamm, who later became Colorado governor, turned those heroes into villains by creating a groundswell against the Games. Lamm's coalition capitalized on a few issues prevalent in the mind of the populous in 1972, including "…a strong environmentalist movement that began in the '60s… inadequate preparations for funding the Games and growing reports of financial losses from previous Olympics," according to the *Denver Post*.

Organizing committee members vastly underestimated the public sentiment against the Olympics, having convinced IOC members that Coloradoans were behind the measure. After the bid was secured, Denver City councilman Dennis Gallagher surveyed his constituents, and the results were shocking—80 percent were against the potential headache an Olympics might inflict. "The promoters never asked the people how they felt, and the arrogance of some Olympic boosters turned everyone off—they tried to imply you lacked patriotism if you were not for the Olympics," Gallagher said at the time.

Officially snubbed by Denver on November 15, 1972, the IOC turned to Whistler, British Columbia; however, government turnover forced that city to decline the offer as well. Ultimately, the IOC contracted Innsbruck, Austria—the Olympic site in 1964—to host the games once again.

Finger pointing replaced lobbying in the years following as Colorodoans continued to argue the merits of declining the bid. Both sides accused the other of manipulation for personal gain. While the argument is moot at this point, the incident will forever affect the State of Colorado. The United States Olympic Committee asserts that Denver has not been blacklisted from hosting future Games, but Sidney Bullene, who served on the Denver Organizing Committee, opines differently. Bullene told the *Post*, "I don't think the IOC will ever give us the Olympics again. We will never ever see the Olympics here again—not in our lifetimes." Although that outlook seems bleak, it is largely believed that it will be some time before Denver is reconsidered.

Springing into Action

The 1978 Amateur Sports Act enacted by Congress granted the United States Olympic Committee

WINTER SPORTS AND THE OLYMPICS

161

(USOC) exclusive governing rights over Olympic-related sport activities in the United States. Congress' measure also provided a mechanism for recognizing the legitimacy of National Governing Bodies (NGBs) pertaining to each individual sport. That same year, the USOC packed the moving vans and headed for high country, establishing residence in Colorado Springs. The city's offer of 36 acres of land and office buildings enticed the newly christened USOC to leave its previous digs in New York City.

In the 30-odd years since the move, the complex has greatly expanded, now boasting a state-of-the-art training facility. According to the USOC, the complex can provide housing, dining, recreational facilities and other services for up to 557 coaches and athletes at any given time. That same compound is home to 12 NGBs, including USA Swimming, with another 12 located inside the city limits of Colorado Springs. The USOC's migration to Colorado continues to serve as a boon for the Pikes Peak region, with Olympic-related business and organizations providing $215 million in annual revenue and roughly 2100 jobs.

Parsing the data further, the USOC and NGBs directly employ 719 people and pay a total tax receipt of $4.9 million to the region. By attracting over 13,000 athletes to the facility, the local economy gained another $15 million in out-of-facility expenditures. Additionally, there are 90 sport-related businesses in the region's sport sector, 50 of which work on USOC-related business on a regular basis.

Notwithstanding, debate continues over the location as detractors point to the facility's relatively long distance from America's population centers and that its position 6000 feet above sea level is counterintuitive to the generally accepted practice of "living high and training low." The reverse occurs in Colorado Springs, where athletes living at sea level are forced to train in the thin air of Colorado, which does not allow for maximum training potential. Signaling confidence in the city, in 2010, the USOC cut the ribbon on a new $53-million facility that will keep the organization in Colorado Springs for the next 30 years.

X-Games at Home in Colorado

Colorado is best described as one of North America's premier winter sports destinations, with nearly 29,000 skiable acres, 11 million visitors annually and $2.6 billion of revenue generated each year. Therefore, it seemed only fitting that in 2002, the Winter X-Games established permanent residence in the Centennial State. The competition is hosted annually in Aspen, one of the state's top tourist destinations, offering access to every winter sport imaginable. In 2002, Aspen's first year as host, the Winter X-Games drew 40,000 people in attendance, making it the largest event the city has ever hosted. Amazed, David Perry of the Aspen Ski Company observed, "The atmosphere was electric. There was definitely more youth in town. It reminded me of Aspen of old. Aspen 20 years ago was full of youthful energy and it became that way again. It was tremendous." The droves frequenting Aspen are treated to far more than the high-flying festivities, as concerts and other youth-centered cultural events fill the slate.

The type of alternative sports culture that Colorado fosters also fits perfectly with the very ideology of the X-Games—going higher, going faster and continually pushing the envelope of conventional sport. It's no secret the event is continually growing both in terms of spectators and television viewers, especially when you consider that in 2009, the Rocky Mountain ski region attracted one-third of all skiers and snowboarders in the United States, a majority of them aged 24 years or younger. Additionally, the mountains of Colorado have always served as a sort of unconventional winter sport laboratory, and each year Winter-X provides tremendous results in the form of the most unique and gravity-defying competition humanly possible, though that definition is constantly evolving.

Teeming with Talent

The Rocky Mountain region played a major role in the 2002 winter sport scene, playing host to the Winter X-Games in Aspen, while subsequently inviting the world to the XIX Winter Olympics in Salt Lake City, Utah. Although Colorado had previously hosted the Winter X-Games in Crested Butte, 2002 was the first time in Aspen—and the new location proved to be just one of many headlines of potentially the Winter X-Games' biggest year. The biggest news was made by the entire 2002 U.S. Olympic snowboard freestyle team, which decided to warm up for Salt Lake City by competing in the Winter-X snowboard superpipe event just weeks before the Olympics got underway.

Critics of the move were concerned that injuries might occur so close to the biggest event in the world, but as the results showed, the risk proved worth the reward. That's because Ross Powers, Danny Kass and J.J. Thomas, all competitors at 2002 Winter-X, finished gold, silver and bronze, respectively, in the Olympic halfpipe competition. It was the first time a nation had swept the podium in that event and was the first all-American Winter Olympics medal sweep since men's figure skating in 1956. Not to be outdone, American Kelly Clark followed up her 2002 Winter-X halfpipe gold with an Olympic gold medal in the same event.

Fans were also treated to 15-year-old Shaun White's first Winter-X medal haul in just his third competition. White took silver in both the slopestyle and superpipe events in 2002 and hasn't failed to podium in Aspen since then, winning 15 medals (10 gold, three silver, two bronze) over the past nine years. Barrett Christy provided another highlight, winning her tenth Winter-X medal with a bronze in women's slopestyle. The bronze was Christy's last medal, but she remains the most decorated woman in Winter-X

WINTER SPORTS AND THE OLYMPICS   165

history. The 2002 version of the Winter-X Games was quite spectacular indeed, but there have been many other amazing moments in the event's history. Here are a few:

- 1998: Winter-X makes its debut in Crested Butte after a one-year stint in Big Bear Lake, California. Crested Butte hosted again in 1999, but the event didn't return to Colorado until Aspen in 2002.
- 2006: Revolving three times over the earth, Jeaux Hall lands the first-ever 1080 in the halfpipe competition. It took a whopping 17 attempts. That same year, ESPN and Aspen sign a contract extension cementing the city as host until 2010.
- 2007: Aspen's own Peter Olenick nails the first Whiskey Flip (a double flip) in halfpipe competition history. It was a fitting achievement for Olenick, who made history at the very same location, Buttermilk Mountain, where he grew up skiing and snowboarding.
- 2009: American Levi LaVallee attempts, and almost lands, a double back flip on a snowmobile. LaVallee successfully completed both rotations, but at the last second was forced to abort the trick, thus not finishing the landing. Shaun White also becomes the first to win back-to-back golds in the snowboard superpipe.

Creating Gold in Silverton

Apparently the cure for humdrum, already-been-seen-before snowboard routines reads as follows. Secure $500,000 from a lucrative sponsor, hire a helicopter, add the world's premier snowboarder in Shaun White and drop them all into a remote ski sanctum in the San Juans of Silverton. That was the exact scenario when global super-brands Red Bull and Oakley partnered to execute "Project X" in 2009, covertly manufacturing a full-size, 540-foot training halfpipe in the backcountry of the Colorado Mountains. The aim was to provide a secluded, state-of-the-art location for Shaun White and other brand-sponsored riders to take the sport to another level.

Project X was born out of the doldrums that struck snowboarding between the 2006 Torino Olympics and 2008 Winter X-Games as boarders were churning out stock routines with no new, explosive elements.

The new pipe granted White full freedom to attempt tricks that only existed in riders' dreams. "I've had all these tricks in my mind I wanted to try. I just needed a place to figure them out," White remarked. For six weeks in February and March 2009, White honed in on the Switch Back 900, the Double Back Rodeo, the Cab Double Cork Ten and the vaunted Double McTwist 1260 (consisting of two flips and three-and-a-half spins).

To produce optimum conditions, the pipe was outfitted with a foam pit that allowed White to perfect his new tricks without fear of injury. Plus, creators situated the halfpipe far from human reach to ensure the athletes' full reign and optimum focus. Only a helicopter or snowmobile granted a person access to the halfpipe. Jen Brill with the city of Silverton ensured the area remained completely exclusive for Shaun and company: "Our guests got to ski the terrain above the pipe, but we kept the guests out of the pipe. A few lucky guests got to see him ride but not many, as it was top secret."

The half-million-dollar experiment worked in spades as White barnstormed the subsequent U.S. Grand Prix circuit, winning four out of the five Grand Prix events that season largely on the merits of the new McTwist 1260, which he officially unveiled in Park City, Utah. White's Grand Prix greatness earned him a spot on the United States' Olympic Snowboard Team, which was largely a formality. At that point it was on to Aspen and the 2010 Winter X-Games where the "Flying Tomato" defended his halfpipe title, becoming the first rider to ever win the event in three consecutive years.

White capped-off his scintillating snowboard season at the 2010 Vancouver Winter Olympic Games, where he entered as the clear-cut favorite in the men's halfpipe competition. After he secured the gold medal with a conservative first run of 45.8 without using the Double McTwist, everyone expected to see the sport's new crown jewel on display in White's final run. Shaun did not disappoint the thousands gathered at Cypress Mountain or the millions watching worldwide, throwing and landing the Double McTwist and in the process improving on his first run. The final run earned a 48.6, the highest Olympic snowboard score ever, making White the back-to-back Olympic gold medalist in halfpipe. In an interview following the record-setting run, White said confidently, "I just felt like I didn't come all the way to Vancouver not to pull out the big guns. I put down the tricks I've worked so hard on."

Project X paid off for all those involved—sponsors, riders and fans alike. Now Colorado awaits an opportunity to aid Shaun White, or any other athlete, in creating the world's next big trick.

Chapter Seven

Outdoor Sports

Running "Bouldly"

Traditional sports often dominate headlines in Colorado, though the fervency for individual sport is not lacking in the least. Colorado's thin air is particularly enticing to distance runners because the altitude increases a person's oxygen capacity and thus creates elite endurance runners. Evidence of running's popularity is played out annually on the streets of Boulder where runners participate in the "Bolder Boulder," the second largest 10K race in the country behind the Peachtree Road Race held in Atlanta.

With 54,000 racers in 2010, Boulder's event is slightly smaller than its Georgian counterpart, but that didn't keep *Runner's World* from naming it America's best 10K road race. Participants race through the heart of Boulder accompanied by the area's picturesque surroundings and finish their journey at the University of Colorado's Folsom Field. There, competitors and onlookers alike participate in one of the largest Memorial Day tributes of its kind. Past winners include the famed 1972 Olympic marathon gold medalist Frank Shorter and 2004 Athens marathon bronze medalist Deena Kastor (née Drossin). The world's greatest runners, along with thousands of other athletes, descend upon Boulder each year, making the race a true destination event.

Leadville 100

Call it a challenge or call it insanity, but no matter what name it's given, the Leadville Trail 100 can only be described as one of the most arduous and demanding ultra-marathon races in the world. Held every year since 1983, "The Race Across The Sky," as it is known, takes place in the once booming mining town of Leadville.

As the mining industry declined, Leadville followed suit, prompting Ken Chlouber to create the event in an attempt to draw visitors and boost the local economy. Today, Leadville thrives again, attracting the world's best athletes annually along with throngs of ultra-marathon race fans. The tremendous toll of traversing 100 miles notwithstanding, the true grind of the LT 100 is found in the extreme altitude gains that racers face throughout the 15-plus-hour event. The participants, more aptly described as warriors, climb and descend a total of 15,600 feet (having elevations of 9200 to 12,620 feet) during the race, and less than half who start actually finish under the 30-hour time limit. For the record, North Carolina's Matt Carpenter set the men's best in 2005 at 15:42:00, while California's Ann Trason's 1994 time of 18:06:24 is the women's standard.

Agonizing Ascent

The Pikes Peak Marathon, the third oldest marathon in the country (and certainly the hardest), began in 1956 as a challenge from three smokers to 10 non-smokers. Today, it remains as America's greatest challenge. Runners climb 7700 feet throughout the event and spend an excruciating portion trudging at altitudes above 12,000 feet, where it can take 30 minutes to complete a single mile. In a flat-level marathon, elite runners finish in just over two hours, but the record at Pikes Peak (3:16:39) is a full hour longer, all thanks to the altitude, steep-switchbacked slopes and rugged terrain. Times do vary, however, as extreme heat and cold, and snow and rain, have all been known to wreak havoc on racers.

Another popular variation of the race, the Pikes Peak Ascent, consists of all the difficulty and none of the nonsense. This shorter version challenges runners to sprint and scurry 13.3 miles, climbing the same 7700 feet in the process. As a testament to its difficulty, the best runners finish this virtual half marathon in the same time it takes to complete a regular sea-level marathon. Not surprisingly, none of the three smokers finished the race in 1956.

For Cyclists Too

The Leadville brand started with just one route, 45 ambitious runners and the vision to change a wayward town; just 38 years later, there are 10 separate races taking place under the Leadville banner. Runners can now try their hand at easier races such as the Leadville 10K or the run-of-the-mill Leadville Marathon—quick jaunts when compared to the original 100-mile standard. For cycling enthusiasts, Leadville added the Leadville Trail 100 Mountain Bike Race in 1994—a simple product extension of the original, but now the subject of worldwide media coverage as a result of the participation of members of the sport's elite: Lance Armstrong, Levi Leipheimer, Dave Wiens and Floyd Landis.

Celebrity cyclist participation in the race led to the documentary film, *Race Across the Sky*, which followed competitors through the grueling 100-mile ordeal in 2009. Similar to the runners, bikers are forced to navigate over 14,000 feet of vertical climb at almost two miles above sea level. Although a majority of the 1500-plus entrants never finish ahead of the 12-hour time limit, the world's best amaze with times in the six-hour range. In August 2010, Leipheimer crushed the previous course record of 6:28:50 set by Armstrong in 2009, with a new time of 6:16:37. Upon crossing the finish line, Leipheimer, who is accustomed to the most extreme racing, gasped, "This is ridiculously hard!" There's no prize money associated with the race, so Leipheimer received what all other

OUTDOOR SPORTS

winners are given: a silver medal, the winners' belt buckle and the pride that comes with conquering the course. Undoubtedly, Ken Chlouber has succeeded in not only putting the once-proud Leadville back on the map, but also in creating some of the world's most challenging, yet wildly popular ultra-races.

Six-shooter in Leadville

A member of the Mountain Biking Hall of Fame, Dave Wiens (of Denver and Gunnison) is best known for his six-straight Leadville Trail 100 Mountain Bike victories from 2003 to 2008. Remarkably, he was the first to break the race's seven-hour mark in 2007, in the process edging Floyd Landis by roughly two minutes for the victory.

A year later, Wiens beat Lance Armstrong for his sixth-straight Leadville title. The two men had been working together throughout the race, drafting and charging forward, until Armstrong ran out of gas, gasping the words, "No. Go. I'm done." Armstrong redeemed himself in 2009, winning the race ahead of Wiens and breaking his six-year reign.

Red Zinger

Celestial Seasonings Herbal Tea Company, based in Boulder, created the "Red Zinger Bicycle Classic" in 1975 as a marketing ploy to promote its new "Red Zinger Tea" and to highlight the alternative modes of transportation in the area. What started as a modest three-day race in the early days became a sensation when Coors Brewing Company took over sponsorship in 1980.

For the next nine years, the world's best descended upon Colorado, California, Nevada, Wyoming and Hawaii to compete in what came to be known as the "Coors International Bicycle Classic" and unofficially America's national tour. Expanded to a two-week stage race, it evolved into the fourth largest cycling race in the world behind the Tour de France, Giro d'Italia and Vuelta a España.

The race is credited for expanding cycling in the American consciousness along with establishing many firsts, three of which include being the highest participation women's race in the world; launching the career of three-time Tour de France winner, Greg LeMond; and being the first event to close a U.S. National Park (Colorado National Monument). The race ended in 1988, but plans to revive stage racing in Colorado were announced in August 2010 by former Colorado governor Bill Ritter and Lance Armstrong. The newly fashioned Quiznos Pro Challenge is scheduled to take place over seven days in August 2011.

Montezuma's Revenge

Imagine racing for 24 hours straight, continually climbing and descending a 14,000-foot mountain for a total of 240 miles and having no finish line to cross. The now defunct Montezuma's Revenge (as of 2006) was just that, requiring participants to navigate Grays

Peak in Colorado's Front Range. Participants pushed themselves for 24 hours (unless they quit) on the most extreme mountain biking course combined with stretches where racers strapped bikes to their backs and scrambled up the steepest portions of the mountain. Although organizers altered the course from year to year, the athletes typically covered 240 miles, while climbing a total of 36,000 vertical feet in the oxygen-depleted, razor-thin Rocky Mountain air. The racer to cover the most distance at the end of those 24 hours was crowned the victor.

Bigger and Boulder

Boulder's many mountain trails appear to be a normal mode of fitness and exercise until you recognize the endurance athletes who train on them, making these paths virtual red carpets for the outdoor sport elite. Besides the high altitude, Boulder's mild weather, close proximity to the Rockies and easy-going disposition make it tailor-made for ultra-athletes seeking the perfect training ground.

American running icon Frank Shorter began training in Boulder in 1970, a move that propelled him to marathon gold at the 1972 Munich Olympics and silver at the 1976 Montreal Games. Boulder is also home to the Phinneys. Davis Phinney is a cycling bronze medalist from the 1984 Olympics and one of 10 Americans to ever win a stage at the Tour de France. His wife, Connie Carpenter-Phinney, won Olympic gold in the 1984 women's mass start and competed in speed skating at the 1972 Winter Olympics in Sapporo. Now their son, Taylor, is the star, already the winner of 22 national and international track cycling events at the age of 21. You may also run into Andy Hampsten on the mountain trails, the 1988 Giro d'Italia Champion and Alpe d'Huez Stage winner at the 1992 Tour de France. The winner of the inaugural 1984 women's Tour de France, Marianne Martin, calls Boulder home as well.

Boulder's A-List Athletes

Boulder is known to offer the perfect accommodation for triathletes, not just for its altitude and trails but also for the several training pools found within the city's borders. It is for these reasons that 1989 Ironman Champion Mark Allen lives and trains in Boulder. Suffice it to say the hills of Boulder are teeming with the world's best. It's difficult to name them all, but here is a list of the most notable:

Mike Pigg: U.S. Triathlon Series Champion.

Colleen Cannon: U.S. Triathlon Series Champion.

Arturo Barrios (Mexico): One-time 10,000-meter world record holder.

Ingrid Kristiansen (Norway): One-time women's world record holder in five different disciplines including the 5000 meters, 10,000 meters and marathon.

Scott Molina: 1988 Ironman Champion.

Erin Baker (New Zealand): 1987 and 1990 Women's Ironman Champion. Named "Triathlete of the Decade" for the 1990s by *Triathlete Magazine.*

Priscilla Welch (UK): Former world record holder for the Women's Masters (40 years plus) Triathlon.

Anton Krupicka: Two-time Leadville Trail 100 winner, along with winning several other ultra-marathons.

Jeremy Horgan-Kobelski: a graduate of the University of Colorado, "JHK" won four national cross-county cycling national championships and received a degree in applied mathematics. He is a 14-time National Champion, member of the U.S. Olympic Team and a fixture on podiums worldwide.

Rob de Castella (Australia): 1983 World Marathon Championship winner and 1986 Boston Marathon Champion.

Rosa Mota (Portugal): Gold medalist in the marathon at the 1988 Seoul Olympics.

Steve Jones (Wales): Former world-record holder in the marathon.

Famed 14ers

Colorado is home to 53 (although some experts contend 54) of the 88 "Fourteeners" found in the United States. The term "fourteener," or "14er," is a colloquial term reserved for a mountain with 14,000 feet of elevation and at least a 300-foot difference in elevation from the next closest peak.

With 53 of the 546 "14ers" worldwide, Colorado boasts 10 percent of the globe's tallest peaks. Hikers, bikers and avid outdoor athletes alike flock to Colorado in hopes of summiting every one of these 14ers, a truly rigorous endeavor. These famed geographical gargantuans are so popular that the NBA's Developmental League team, located in Broomfield, was named the "Colorado 14ers" during its brief, three-year stint.

At 14,433 feet, Mount Elbert in the Sawatch Range is Colorado's tallest peak, followed by Sawatch Range neighbor Mount Massive (14,421) and, just one foot shorter, Mount Harvard (14,420) of the Collegiate Range.

Although some climb Colorado's peaks leisurely, others turn the task into competition. There are several official and unofficial speed records pertaining to climbing these behemoths, including Todd Keizer's record-setting completion of every Colorado 14er in a jaw-dropping 10 days, 20 hours and 26 minutes.

Outdoor Sports Notes

• From the mountain-biking hotbed of Durango, Travis Brown was a 2006 inductee to the Mountain Bike Hall of Fame. Brown has accomplished everything a person can on a mountain bike, most notably representing the U.S. at the 2000 Olympics, winning two Single Speed World Championships, five Colorado State Cyclocross Championships and the

1999 National Off-Road Bicycle Association (NORBA) XC title.

- Mountain bike champion Ned Overend moved to Durango when he was 27 and launched his professional cycling career shortly afterward. Overend's phenomenal tenure produced six overall NORBA titles as well as 14 other individual and cumulative championships (among numerous other achievements and honors), including the gold medal at the first-ever Union Cycliste Internationale (UCI) World Championship in 1990. Nicknamed "The Lung" for his incredible aerobic ability, Overend is a member of the Mountain Bike Hall of Fame and U.S. Bicycling Hall of Fame.

- The International Mountain Biking Association (IMBA), based in Boulder, is the largest non-profit mountain biking advocacy group of its kind, attempting to "...create, enhance and preserve great trail experiences for mountain bikers worldwide." IMBA continually aims to "...encourage low-impact riding, volunteer trailwork participation, cooperation among different trail user groups, grassroots advocacy and innovative trail management solutions."

Chapter Eight

Colorado Sports Icons

The Manassa Mauler

Born in the small southwestern town of Manassa in 1895, William Harrison Dempsey, aka, Jack Dempsey, grew up poor and traveled often because his father needed to look for work. There was not much work to be had for an uneducated son of parents of mixed ancestry (Jack's grandfather was Irish, and his grandmother was half Cherokee). During his lifetime, Dempsey worked as a ditch-digger, peach-picker, lumberjack and circus entertainer, but as a teenager he quickly discovered that his muscular frame and steel jaw were excellent for fighting. So to make money, he traveled from town to town, visiting saloons and challenging any takers to a fight. If anyone was foolish enough to accept, bets were wagered and the fight would begin. His barroom brawls eventually earned him a following, and Dempsey entered the professional ring.

He began his early, nomadic boxing journey at the age of 16 training at Young Peter Jackson's Gym in

Salt Lake City. His first professional fight was under the name "Kid Blackie" in 1914, and he began racking up victory after victory in small, dank venues across the American west. Dempsey delighted fans with his heavy-handed knockouts, quickly making a name for himself as a big-time boxer capable of winning the sport's ultimate crown. Just as soon as he built a robust reputation in the ring, World War I broke out and he began working in a naval shipyard assembling and manufacturing the machines of war. Public sentiment at the time was that Dempsey had dodged army service, but in 1920 he proved that he was rejected by the U.S. Army. After the war, he slowly made his way back to the ring, where he amassed a professional record of 58 wins, 11 losses and 4 draws by the year 1919 when he was finally offered a shot at the title.

Dempsey Arrives

On Independence Day 1919, Dempsey went toe-to-toe with the current world champion at the time, Jess Willard, also known as the "Great White Hope" after he took the heavyweight title from the renowned Jack Johnson in 1915. The bout, considered a match-up of David and Goliath because of Willard's larger stature, was fraught with controversy as Dempsey won by TKO in the fourth round after dismantling his opponent's face. Willard was knocked down seven times, all in the first round, and his corner prohibited their fighter from answering the fourth round bell. By that time, Willard's face was severely disfigured as Dempsey allegedly broke some of his facial bones, including Willard's jaw and a few teeth, as well as numerous ribs. An eyewitness account from Dempsey's discontented former manager Jack Kearns (who had been fired) espoused the "loaded gloves" theory, stating that the fighter's hand wrappings were made out of plaster of Paris. If true, such a method of cheating would have provided the already heavy punching Dempsey with lethal weapons. Others contend that in the first round, Dempsey used an implement akin to a railroad tie to repeatedly mangle and skewer his opponent.

Since the countless years following the 1919 title bout, detractors and proponents of Dempsey have argued the merits of his victory, but no conclusive evidence exists in either case. Ultimately, Dempsey's TKO win over Willard made him the Heavyweight Champion of the World, a title he held for the next seven years.

During that seven-year stretch, Dempsey successfully defended his title four times, and his 1921 tilt with Frenchman Georges Carpantier generated the first million-dollar gate receipt in boxing history as 91,000 fans attended Boyle's Thirty Acres in Jersey City, New Jersey. Dempsey's sixth title defense came against Gene Tunney, who proved too strong for the "Manassa Mauler"; Tunney won the title bout by way of unanimous decision after 10 rounds. The city of Philadelphia hosted the fight and saw a new record crowd of 120,557—only soccer and auto racing ever saw a larger crowd. When explaining to his wife the reason for his defeat, Dempsey reportedly quipped, "I forgot to duck," a line also delivered by President Reagan to his wife after being shot in an assassination attempt in 1981.

Upon losing his heavyweight title, Dempsey stepped into the ring just twice more, beating Jack Sharkey at Yankee Stadium in June 1927 and losing a title rematch to Tunney in September later that year.

Despite his unsuccessful effort at recapturing the belt, Dempsey finished his career with a spectacular 66 wins (51 by KO), 6 losses and 11 draws. In retirement, he served in the military during World War II and tried his hand at several other endeavors, including running a restaurant, writing books and making continual public appearances to meet fans. Dempsey was inducted into the Boxing Hall of Fame in 1990 and is considered *The Ring's* 10th greatest heavyweight of all time and the seventh greatest puncher ever. Although he never returned to his humble roots in Manassa, Jack Dempsey will always remain the state's greatest boxing champion.

Jack Dempsey Quotations and Facts

"A champion is someone who gets up when he can't."

"A champion owes everybody something. He can never pay back for all the help he got, for making him an idol."

"Tall men come down to my height when I hit 'em in the body."

"All the time he's boxing, he's thinking. All the time he was thinking, I was hitting him."

On his deathbed, Dempsey told his wife, Deanna, "Don't worry honey; I'm too mean to die."

In 1950, Dempsey published a book on boxing called *Championship Fighting: Explosive Punching and Aggressive Defense*. The book emphasized knockout power through the movement of one's bodyweight. His book was a great influence on Bruce Lee.

Glenn Morris: Olympic Hero

Born on his family's horse ranch near Simla, Glenn Morris showed early promise in athletics. Entering Colorado Agricultural College (now Colorado State University) in 1930, Morris became a star athlete for the school in several sports but excelled in track and field. After finishing school, he worked as an assistant track coach and an automobile salesman, but he still burned for competition. In 1934, he decided to begin training in the decathlon in the hopes of making the 1936 Olympics.

At the U.S. Olympic track trials, Morris did more than simply qualify; he set a new world record in the decathlon with 7880 points. Once the press got wind of the story, Morris became the talk of the country leading up to the 1936 Olympics to the point that *Newsweek* dubbed him, "the nation's new Iron Man." By the time Morris had made the trip to Berlin for the start of the Olympics, he had competed in just two full decathlons.

But none of that mattered during the competition. It was said that while Morris was on the field, Adolf Hitler never left the stadium, so enraptured was he with the American athlete. Morris had completed all the events and was left with the 1500-meter race to finish. He had already secured himself the gold medal; all he needed to do was complete the run in 4:34 seconds and he would break his own world record. As Morris ran around the track, the German crowd urged him on through the last few meters, and when he crossed the line with a time of 4:33.2, he had secured the gold medal and a new world record. At the medal ceremony, Morris received his gold from Hitler's mistress, Eva Braun.

The Germans were so enthralled by Morris' performance that they offered him $50,000 to stay in Berlin and appear in sports films. An athlete with a chiseled jaw and impressive physique, Morris would have made an excellent subject for the German propaganda films of director Leni Riefenstahl, but Morris refused the offer and returned to the U.S.

Morris might have rejected the offer to stay in Germany, but that did not stop him, according to Leni Riefenstahl's 1987 autobiography, from having a lurid affair with her during his stay in Berlin. Of particular interest is Riefenstahl's description of the medal ceremony, which she describes with vivid detail and great imagination.

"The dim light prevented any filming of the ceremony, and when Glenn Morris came down the steps he headed straight towards me. I held out my hand and congratulated him, but he grabbed me in his arms, tore off my blouse and kissed my breasts, right in the middle of the stadium, in front of a hundred thousand spectators. A lunatic, I thought. I wrenched myself out of his grasp and dashed away. But I could not forget the wild look in his eyes."

The account was entertaining but was complete fiction. Had something like that occurred in Germany to Hitler's favorite director, Morris might not have returned to the United States.

Upon his arrival on U.S. soil, Morris was given a ticker-tape parade in New York City and received a hero's welcome in Colorado. With his rugged good looks and the fame of the Olympics still fresh in people's minds, Hollywood came calling, hoping to cash in on Morris' popularity, and they cast him in two films, *Tarzan's Revenge* and *Hold That Co-Ed*. Neither film was a success. Morris then tried his hand at professional sports, playing one game for the Detroit Lions, but he sustained an injury in his first game that permanently took him out of athletics. When World War II broke out, Morris served in the U.S. Navy and was stationed in the Pacific commanding amphibious assault landing crafts. He returned to civilian life and worked in a variety of jobs before living out his last days in a veteran's hospital in California. He died on January 31, 1974.

Simla High School honors his legacy to this day with an annual Glenn Morris Award for athletic and academic excellence.

Dean Lahr

Denver native Dean Lahr was a natural-born athlete. Out of high school he was already a decorated three-sport athlete in football, wrestling and track and field. Because of his skills in the arena of sport, he received full scholarship to the University of Colorado and proved himself both on the field and in the classroom. But wrestling was his true passion, and after dropping all other sports, from 1962 to 1964 he was not only one of the most dominant wrestlers in the U.S. but also in the world. Over a three-year period, he lost only two matches and won 42. One of his losses came at the hands of the 1960 Olympic champion from Turkey.

As the 1964 Tokyo Olympics neared, Lahr was considered one of the top chances for a U.S. medal in wrestling, but just two months before the Olympic trials began, he tore his anterior cruciate ligament in his leg. Despite his injuries he was determined to compete and not lose out on his dream. He managed to recover enough to compete and win his weight class and was named top wrestler at the trials.

Unfortunately, Lahr injured himself yet again during the trials and missed out on a trip to the Japan Olympics. After recovering for nearly two years, he returned to competitive amateur wrestling, winning a national wrestling title in 1966 and competing at the World Championship that same year, where he beat out a Russian and an Austrian, drew with the three-time world champion for Iran and lost to a wrestler from Turkey.

Dean Lahr gave up wrestling in the late 1960s and eventually opened up a business in Honduras. He was inducted into the Colorado Sports Hall of Fame in 2010.

In Full Bloom

Some athletes simply excel on raw talent and others succeed based on drive. And then there is Jeremy Bloom, who emanated both characteristics from every pore of his body. It's difficult to choose a starting point when describing Bloom's career, but that's not uncommon with such an accomplished multi-sport superstar.

At 5 feet 9 inches and 180 pounds, the Loveland native used his speed to run right past the critics who said he could not play football. Bloom's high school football team won the Colorado High School Championship his senior year, largely based on his speed and shiftiness as a receiver and kick-returner. For many athletes, a state title would complete their high school career, but for Bloom it was just another item in an asset-filled balance sheet. That's because at age 15, Bloom doubled as an elite freestyle skier, the youngest to ever join the United States freestyle ski team at the time.

COLORADO SPORTS ICONS

Following high school, Bloom signed a letter of intent with the University of Colorado to play football in Boulder, but he took a year in between to focus on his Olympic dream. In that World Cup season, Bloom became the youngest freestyle World Cup Champion in history. He went on to realize his dream of competing at the Salt Lake City Olympics, finishing ninth. A year later in 2002, Bloom commenced a short but stellar career with the Colorado Buffaloes. In just two years, he scored five touchdowns of 75 yards or more, tying the legendary Byron White in Colorado's record book. Bloom also holds the Colorado record for longest touchdown from scrimmage, with a 94-yard score versus Kansas State on October 5, 2002.

Bloom continued his skiing career on the World Cup circuit, and he began receiving sponsorship as he ramped up training for the 2006 Torino Olympics. The NCAA disapproved, and a two-year battle over Bloom's collegiate eligibility ensued with the governing body ruling against Bloom. Although his college football days came to an end, Bloom focused on skiing, and in 2005 he won a record six-straight World Cup events in a single season. He finished a disappointing sixth in Torino, but in total, he laid claim to three World Championships and 11 World Cup Golds during his skiing career. Following Torino, the NFL's Philadelphia Eagles drafted Bloom in 2006, but he never saw game action as he was plagued by injuries. Today, Bloom is focused on his philanthropic efforts, directing the Wish of a Lifetime Foundation, which focuses on fulfilling the lifelong dreams of low-income seniors.

Chapter Nine

Sports Potpourri

The Colorado Rapids

In Major League Soccer's (MLS) 15-year existence, only three postseason own goals have occurred and just one ever decided a match's outcome. Apparently, destiny joined the Rapids' side in 2010 as the most recent own goal in MLS Cup history came in overtime of the finals, delivering Colorado its first league title.

The deciding tally deflected off the thigh of FC Dallas defender George John 17 minutes into overtime. Colorado substitute Macoumba Kandji took a long pass in the box from Conor Casey, and after eluding one defender with a nifty nutmeg, he crossed the ball across the goal-front in hopes of connecting with oncoming teammates. At precisely the same moment, John came to the rescue of his badly beaten teammate but inadvertently redirected the ball into his own net after his goaltender Kevin Hartman had already committed his body to the other side of the net.

The play left the heavily favored FC Dallas side stunned in disbelief. Colorado was equally shocked following the go-ahead goal, but theirs was a feeling of elation. The two sides played 13 more pressure-packed minutes of soccer that night in Toronto, but it was not enough time for FC Dallas to overcome its devastating defensive gaff earlier in the match. Colorado emerged a 2–1 victor and champions of MLS.

Not all goals are created equal, but they are almost always the result of desire and will. Kandji's effort and the resulting own goal were the direct byproduct of his attempt to create a scoring chance. Former United States defender Alexi Lalas, who called the finale for ESPN, was very clear in his assessment: "There's nothing beautiful about this goal except for the fact that it wins Colorado their MLS Cup. You got to have a little bit of luck, but you also have to take people on."

Following the game, Rapids manager Gary Smith explained how his players forced fate's hand vis-à-vis the conclusive goal: "The overriding thought has to be that, in order for somebody to score an own goal, they must be under some pressure to make that mistake...I'm just pleased that the guys were able to, in that extra time, mount enough of an attack to make a difference."

The manner by which the game finished was just as unexpected as Colorado's run to the MLS Cup finals. The Rapids spent much of the regular season mired in mediocrity, and at season's end found themselves in fifth position in the Western Conference with 12 wins, 8 losses and 10 ties. The record resulted in 46 total points, barely qualifying Colorado as the seventh seed in the eight-team playoff draw. The Conference semifinals pitted the boys from Denver against the perennially strong Columbus Crew. Colorado blanked Columbus 1–0 at home in the first leg of the home-and-away series. In the second match, Colorado trailed 2–0 late in the second half looking for any way to pot a goal and force the series into extra time based on aggregate goals. Then, in the 84th minute, Colorado's leading man, Conor Casey, drew a goal back from Columbus, and by the final whistle, the two teams had each scored two goals during the series.

After a scoreless 30-minute overtime period, penalties were used to advance one of the teams. Colorado shot first, and between the two teams, the first nine players scored, putting immense pressure on Columbus' Brian Carroll to score and continue the shootout. As Carroll approached the ball, Colorado netminder Matt Pickens startled his opponent, and the ball sailed harmlessly over the crossbar, advancing Colorado deeper into the playoffs.

The next round proved much easier for Colorado as the team negotiated a 1–0 win at home against the eighth-seeded San Jose Earthquakes, earning the Rapids a bid to the final game against FC Dallas. From there, Colorado's 2010 Cinderella story became complete, thanks to the tenacity of Macoumba Kandji and good fortune by way of George John.

Of special note, Rapids' forward Conor Casey was born in New Hampshire but grew up in Denver. He played high school soccer at Denver's South High School. Although he was originally allocated to Toronto, he was traded to the Colorado Rapids in 2007 and became the team's all-time leading goal scorer in 2010. Moreover, Casey was named the MLS Cup MVP for his efforts in leading the Rapids to their first-ever title.

Beckham Unveiled

The 2007 MLS All-Star event at Dick's Sporting Goods Park served as the backdrop of one of the league's greatest showcase events in its history—the unveiling of its newest superstar, David Beckham. The global soccer icon signed a five-year mega deal with the Los Angeles Galaxy in 2007, foregoing a two-year extension with Real Madrid after waning talent relegated him to limited playing time.

Beckham's move to MLS was a calculated maneuver designed to increase the league's profile, attract sponsorship dollars and grow the sport of soccer in America. Beckham was aware of the business plan, stating, "The main thing for me is to improve the soccer, to improve the standard, and to be part of history really because I think soccer can be a lot bigger in the U.S."

Because of the nature of the deal he was under with Real Madrid, Beckham could not join his new Galaxy squad when the 2007 season commenced. He was forced to wait until midsummer when his contract terminated in Spain. In his first, official public viewing on July 13, Beckham was paraded in front of 5000 fans and upwards of 700 accredited journalists at the Home Depot Center, where the Galaxy play their home matches.

But Beckham's real coming-out party came two weeks later at the MLS All-Star game at Dick's Sporting Goods Park just outside Denver. The MLS's newest icon was introduced to the league and the country prior to the game and Beckham took part in an extensive interview at halftime, all on national television. The MLS All-Stars defeated Scotland's Celtic squad 4–0 that night, but all eyes were on David Beckham.

The weekend event simultaneously served as the de facto exhibition of Major League Soccer's newest centerpiece stadium and the Rapid's new home. Dick's Sporting Goods Park was built as an homage to great European stadiums, with an 18,000-seat capacity, luxury seat options, a 360-degree view concourse and state-of-the-art regulation pitch. The stadium is surrounded by 24 practice fields, one of which is an exact replica of the actual game pitch, and the roof panels are fashioned after the tectonic plates that formed the Rocky Mountains. Farther out, several office buildings, restaurants and stores flank the soccer facility. In all, Kroenke Sports and Entertainment refers to the complex as the "Largest professional stadium and fields complex on Earth."

Cooke and Beckham Reunite

David Beckham is the poster boy of former European stars migrating to Major League Soccer for one last hurrah under America's bright spotlight before the curtain goes down on their career. For Beckham's former Manchester United teammate and roommate, Terry Cooke, the MLS offered a second career chance at continuing play after failed attempts to become a permanent fixture at soccer's highest level in England. Both men offered much promise as members of the powerful Manchester United sides of the 1990s, but from that point on their career trajectories took vastly different shapes.

Cooke began his career as the golden boy for United, much more so than Beckham, who struggled for playing time in his early playing days. Regrettably, Cooke's success was rapidly hampered by injury and the frustration that came with loans to lesser clubs across the English countryside. Meanwhile, "Becks," Cooke's former understudy, gained a foothold in the starting 11 and suddenly basked in the glow of international superstardom and prestige that came with starring for the world's favorite club and the English National Team.

After several disappointing English campaigns and relegation to lesser squads, Cooke joined the

Colorado Rapids in 2005 hoping to regain the promise and vitality of his youth. The man who scored the deciding goal in England's 1995 Youth FA Cup and was named Youth Player of the Year, now found himself in a comparatively less than spectacular situation. Meanwhile, in Europe, Beckham was taking the pitch for yet another premier club in Real Madrid of Spain's top league (La Liga) and still enjoying unprecedented fame, whether his play merited the spotlight or not.

Despite both men taking separate paths following their boyhood days at Manchester United, the two men arrived at exactly the same point on March 29, 2008. Again, Dick's Sporting Goods Park in Denver played host to another major David Beckham event, this time the venue for the season opener pitting Beckham's new Los Angeles Galaxy club against Cooke's Colorado Rapids. The two had not seen each other in a fair amount of time, but reunited on the pitch once again, this time under much different circumstances. As if everything came full circle to their earliest days in England, it was Cooke who shined in the reunion match, scoring a goal as part of his Rapids' 4–0 win over Beckham's Galaxy.

Colorado Rapids Facts

- The Denver-based MLS club has changed its logo three times since 1995.
- From 1996 to 2001, the Colorado Rapids played their home games in Mile High Stadium.

- As evidence of soccer's development in the United States, 20 of the 25 players on the Rapids 2010 MLS Cup-winning roster played soccer collegiately.

- The Rapids MLS Cup victory at BMO Field in Toronto was the first MLS championship game played outside the continental U.S.

- Gary Smith, coach of the Rapids 2010 MLS Cup Champion team, is only the fifth English head coach to win a major soccer championship while coaching abroad.

Soccer's Superwoman

Under the captainship of Denver's April Heinrichs, the United States National Women's Soccer Team won the inaugural 1991 Women's World Cup held in China. The former star at the University of North Carolina scored four goals for the U.S. at the tournament, including a two-goal effort against Brazil in the group stage, to lead the United States to a perfect 5–0 record and the first World Cup Title. Throughout her international career, Heinrichs earned 47 caps and 38 goals for the United States and in 1998 became the first woman inducted into the National Soccer Hall of Fame.

Heinrichs' phenomenal career began at Littleton's Heritage High School as the state's best player, leading the Eagles to four league titles and two state championships. Individually, she was named

All-Conference three times, All-State twice and All-American once.

After her time at Heritage, Heinrichs matriculated to play collegiate soccer at powerhouse North Carolina, where she won three national championships and graduated as college soccer's all-time leading scorer (87 goals). She was given All-American First Team honors three times and named National Player of the Year twice while at UNC. During her career, Heinrichs was named U.S. Soccer Athlete of the Year in 1986 and 1989. To add to her list of accomplishments, Heinrichs was named *Soccer America* magazine's Female Player of the 1980s. North Carolina also retired her jersey, making her the first woman to receive this honor in the school's illustrious soccer history.

Heinrichs went on to coach at the collegiate level but eventually joined the Women's National Team as assistant coach from 1995 to 2000 and head coach from 2000 to 2005. In 2006, she was named head coach of the University of California-Irvine Anteaters but vacated the position for a role with the United State Olympic Committee in Colorado Springs. In 2005, Heinrichs was inducted into the Colorado Sports Hall of Fame.

The Rocky Mountain Cup

Climb over several mountain peaks, walk through a handful of valleys, traverse a state and you come to the Colorado Rapids closest rival in Major League Soccer, the Real Salt Lake, of Salt Lake City.

When MLS expanded in 2005, Real Salt Lake became just the second team based in the Rocky Mountain region. To help foster a rivalry between the two clubs, the "Committee of 10," which consists of five supporters belonging to both sides, put forth the idea of the two teams battling for the right to be called the Rocky Mountain champions. The contest was called the Rocky Mountain Cup, and the first game took place on April 16, 2005. The competition is decided over the course of the regular MLS season each time the two clubs meet. The teams are awarded three points for a win and one point for a tie, and at the end of the regular season, the Cup is handed out to the team with the most points.

Although Real Salt Lake won the first game, the Rapids won the subsequent three matches in 2005 and clinched the first Rocky Mountain Cup at their final meeting of the season. The Rapids won the Cup again in 2006, but ever since then, Real Salt Lake has owned the trophy.

The Voice of an Era

Bob Martin, Colorado's best-known broadcaster, was *the* voice of Colorado sports during his storied career. Martin called Bronco football games for 25 years but also performed play-by-play for the University of Colorado, Colorado State and Air Force Football. His basketball duties included the Denver

Rockets, Denver-Chicago Truckers, the AAU Tournament, NCAA finals and University of Colorado. Martin also called Denver Bear baseball games and could be heard nationally describing the action at the US and British Opens, along with PGA Golf.

Fans remember his famous line from basketball broadcasts, saying, "He missed the entire apparatus" when a player shot an air ball. Martin's Bronco broadcasts were legendary, though the team played poorly for many of his years as broadcaster. If anyone asked him, Martin would say his favorite job was with Denver University hockey. He was also involved with election coverage and hosted music programming. Martin's incredible broadcast talents earned him Colorado Broadcaster of the Year honors 22 times, the CBA Broadcaster of the Year Award, election into the Colorado Sports Hall of Fame, the University of Denver Hall of Fame, and a permanent place in the minds of all who listened during that era.

The Colorado Mammoth

In 2006 the National Lacrosse League (NLL) drew one million fans to the box office in a single season for the first time in its 20-year history. Fittingly, the one-millionth fan was at the Pepsi Center to view a playoff tilt between the Colorado Mammoth and Arizona Sting. Since their debut in 2003, the Mammoth consistently led the league in attendance figures, edging out Toronto (where lacrosse is technically the official sport of Canada) to draw the most fans league-wide in just their second season.

Therefore, NLL commissioner Jim Jennings thought it appropriate that the one-millionth-fan honor came at the Pepsi Center in Denver: "We're excited to surpass the one million fans mark in a single season for the first time in league history." Jennings went on to honor Colorado fans directly, stating, "The great fans of the Colorado Mammoth have played a huge role in allowing us to reach this goal." By 2008, the Mammoth draw grew even larger, giving the club a higher average attendance per game than Pepsi Center co-occupants Colorado Avalanche and Denver Nuggets.

Box office figures aren't the Mammoth's only claim to fame—they also produce a high level of talent on display every season. Under the direction of co-owners Stan Kroenke and Broncos legend John Elway, the Mammoth have had only two losing seasons in the eight years they have called Denver home, with Division Championships coming three times (2004, 2006 and 2007). The Mammoth had a phenomenal postseason in 2006 and won the organization's first National Lacrosse League Championship.

Get Your Gait

The Colorado Mammoth retired the jersey number of its greatest player Gary Gait in 2005, making his number 22 the second jersey to be retired in the history of the National Lacrosse League. Additionally, by hanging Gait's jersey from the Pepsi Center rafters, it became the first and only sweater hung anywhere around the NLL.

Gait starred with the Colorado Mammoth from 2003 to 2005 and throughout his 15-year career amassed 596 goals, 495 assists for 1091 points, making him the league's all-time scoring leader at the time of his retirement (a record since surpassed by John Tavares).

After retirement, Gait became the Mammoth head coach for two years and was at the helm for the 2006 championship. Other achievements for Gait during his Mammoth years include NLL Most Valuable Player (2003), NLL Sportsmanship Award (2004, 2005), Regular Season Scoring Leader (2004), Regular Season Goals Leader (2003, 2004). He single-handedly holds every Mammoth franchise record of note.

Gait has since come out of retirement and is playing for the Rochester Knighthawks where his brother, Paul, is the coach. For his extensive accomplishments during his college years, and for being in the professional ranks and for his international play, Gait was inducted into the United States Lacrosse National Hall of Fame and the National Lacrosse League Hall of Fame.

Mammoth Fact

- Over 90 percent of the Colorado Mammoth players were born in Canada.

Notes on Sources

Website Sources

associatedcontent.com/article/39793/john_elway_great_
football_player_great.html?cat=19

cbssports.com/collegefootball/story/14090929/fifth-down-
reverberates-20-years-later-especially-for-missouribolderboulder.com

cctigers.com (Colorado College)

coloradoavalanche.com

coloradomammoth.com

coloradorapids.com

coloradosports.org (Colorado Sports Hall of Fame)

csurams.com (Colorado State University)

cubuffs.com (Colorado Buffaloes)

denverbroncos.com

denverpioneers.com (Denver University)

denverpost.com

espn.com

expn.com (ESPN X-Games)

faqs.org/sports-science/Ha-Ja/High-Altitude-Effects-on-Sport-
Performance.html

goairforcefalcons.com (Air Force Academy)

leadvilletrail100.com/home.aspx (Leadville 100)

lpga.com

milb.com (Minor League Baseball)

mlb.com (Major League Baseball)

mlssoccer.com (Major League Soccer)

nba.com (National Basketball Association)

nba.com/nuggets (Denver Nuggets)

news.google.com/newspapers?id=i0YaAAAAIBAJ&sjid=2Sc
EAAAAIBAJ&pg=4400,3522789&dq=minnesota+north+stars&
hl=en

nfl.com (National Football League

nhl.com (National Hockey League)

nll.com (National Lacrosse League)

NOTES ON SOURCES

pgatour.com

profootballhof.com

olympic.org (International Olympic Committee)

retrosheet.org

rockies.mlb.com (Colorado Rockies)

scores.espn.go.com/mlb/recap?gameId=280417125

skimuseum.net (Colorado Ski and Snowboard Museum)

slate.com/id/2176547/

sports.espn.go.com/espn/wire?section=nfl&id=2744058

sports.espn.go.com/nfl/news/story?id=3471189

sports.espn.go.com/nfl/news/story?id=4409512

sportsillustrated.cnn.com/siforwomen/top_100/39/

sportsillustrated.cnn.com/vault/article/magazine/MAG1136947/index.htm

sports.yahoo.com/nfl/blog/shutdown_corner/post/John-Elway-invested-15-million-in-a-Ponzi-schem?urn=nfl-276931

startribune.com/sports/

startribune.com/sports/wild/12674787.htm

steamboat.com/media (Steamboat Springs Media)

usatoday.com/sports/baseball/nl/rockies/2006-05-30-rockies-cover_x.htm

usatoday.com/sports/baseball/nl/rockies/2007-10-09-humidor2-coors_N.htm

teamusa.org (United States Olympic Committee)

Book Sources

Barton, George. *My Lifetime in Sports*. Minneapolis: Olympic Press, 1958.

Brackin, Dennis and Patrick Reusse. *Minnesota Twins: The Complete Illustrated History*. Minneapolis: MVP Books, an imprint of MBI Publishing and the Quayside Publishing Group, 2010.

Gillete, Gary, ed. *The ESPN Pro Football Encyclopedia,* first edition. New York: Sterling Publishing, 2006.

Hartman, Sid with Joel Rippel. *Sid Hartman's Great Minnesota Sports Moments*. St. Paul, MN: Voyageur Press, an imprint of MBI Publishing, 2006.

Hugunin, Marc and Stew Thornley. *Minnesota Hoops: Basketball in the North Star State*. St. Paul, MN: Minnesota Historical Society Press, 2006.

Johnson, Lloyd and Miles Wolff, ed. *Encyclopedia of Minor League Baseball, third edition*. Durham, N.C.: Baseball America, Inc., 2007.

Johnson, Lloyd, ed. *The Minor League Register*. Durham, NC: Baseball America, Inc., 1994.

Leerhsen, Charles. *Crazy Good: The True Story of Dan Patch, the most famous horse in America*. New York: Simon and Schuster, 2008.

MacCambridge, Michael, ed. *ESPN College Football Encyclopedia: the complete history of the game*. New York: ESPN Books, 2005.

Miller, Jeff. *Going Long. The Wild Ten-Year Saga of the Renegade American Football League in the Words of Those Who Lived It*. New York: McGraw-Hill, 2003.

Oberst, Greg and J. Alexander Poulton. *Washington Sports Trivia*. Montreal: Overtime Books, an imprint of Editions de la Montagne Verte, 2010.

O'Neal, Bill. *The American Association: A Baseball History, 1902–1991*. Austin, Texas: Eakin Press, 1991.

Palmer, Pete and Gary Gillete, ed. *The Baseball Encyclopedia*. New York: Barnes and Noble Books, 2004.

Purdy, Dennis. *The Team by Team Encyclopedia of Major League Baseball.* New York: Workman Publishing, 2006.

Reavis, Tracey. *The Nicknames. The Official NBA Encyclopedia (3rd Edition).* New York: Doubleday, 2000.

Rippel, Joel. *Game of My Life: Minnesota. Memorable Stories of Gophers Football.* Champaign, IL: Sports Publishing, LLC, 2007.

Rippel, Joel. *Minnesota Sports Almanac.* St. Paul, MN: Minnesota Historical Society Press, 2006.

Rippel, Joel. *75 Memorable Moments in Minnesota Sports.* St. Paul, MN: Minnesota Historical Society Press, 2003.

Roberts, Kate. *Minnesota 150. The People, Places and Things That Shape Our State.* St. Paul, MN: Minnesota Historical Society Press, 2007.

Sargent, Scott Allen. *The Complete Historical and Reference Guide to the World Hockey Association, 1972–1979.* Tempe, AZ: Xaler Press, 1995.

Thornley, Stew, ed. *Minnesotans in Baseball.* Minneapolis: Nodin Press, 2009.

Media Guides/Record Books

2007–08 Official NBA Guide

2007–08 Official NBA Register

Minnesota Timberwolves 2008–09 media guide

Minnesota Vikings 2010 media guide

National Baseball Hall of Fame and Museum 2010 Yearbook

NHL Official Guide and Record Book, 2009–10

University of Minnesota 2010 football media and records book

Other Publications

Crossings, a Stearns County History Museum publication. July 2008.

Ryan O'Leary

Ryan O'Leary lives in Boulder. He earned a Bachelor of Journalism degree from the University of Missouri and worked for two years in sport marketing. He attended graduate school at West Virginia University and received a Masters degree in Sport Management, and was hired by NBC Television to work as a researcher for their Olympic Coverage in Beijing. He has freelanced for CTV, NBC, Versus and others. His two favourite sports are baseball and hockey, and he is very passionate about the sporting industry.

J. Alexander Poulton

J. Alexander Poulton is a writer, photographer and genuine sports enthusiast. He's even willing to admit he has "called in sick" during the broadcasts of major sports events so that he can get in as much viewing as possible.

He has earned a BA in English literature and a graduate diploma in journalism, and has over 25 sports books to his credit, including books on hockey, soccer, golf and the Olympics.